W9-BZF-735

Twayne's United States Authors Series

Sylvia E. Bowman, *Editor*

INDIANA UNIVERSITY

Kenneth Burke

Kenneth Burke

By ARMIN PAUL FRANK
Johann Wolfgang Goethe-Universität, Germany

Twayne Publishers, Inc. :: New York

Copyright © 1969 by Twayne Publishers, Inc.
All Rights Reserved

Library of Congress Catalog Card Number: 74-79213

MANUFACTURED IN THE UNITED STATES OF AMERICA

PS
3503
.U6134
Z66

"Ecrire ou parler, c'est user d'une faculté nécessairement commune à tous les hommes, d'une faculté primordiale et inconsciente. On ne peut l'analyser sans faire toute l'anatomie de l'intelligence."

REMY DE GOURMONT,
"Du Style ou de l'Ecriture," 1899

FOR M.P.B.

by desert and earning

Acknowledgments

For permission to quote from his books, I am very much obliged to Mr. Kenneth Burke and his publishers, as follows: Hermes Publications (new editions of *Counter-Statement, Permanence and Change,* and *Attitudes toward History; Book of Moments,* original edition); University of California Press (new edition of *Towards a Better Life; Language as Symbolic Action* and *The Complete Poems: 1915–1967*). Passages from the *Grammar* and *Rhetoric of Motives* are reprinted by permission of George Braziller, Inc.; from the *Rhetoric of Religion* by permission of the Beacon Press, copyright © 1961 by Kenneth Burke.

I am also grateful to the University of Minnesota Press for permission to quote from William H. Rueckert, *Kenneth Burke and the Drama of Human Relations;* to Faber and Faber, Ltd., and to Farrar, Straus & Giroux, Inc., to quote from T. S. Eliot, *On Poetry and Poets*; and to Hans P. Guth, to quote from his unpublished doctoral dissertation, "Threat as the Basis of Beauty: Pragmatist Elements in the Aesthetics of Richards, Dewey, and Burke" (University of Michigan).

Preface

The purpose of the present monograph is to describe, examine, and analyze Kenneth Burke's extant work in its entirety by surveying his fiction and poetry as well as his critical, speculative, and philosophical writings, and by attempting to discover principles common to all of his literary pursuits. This perspective has not been employed on Burke in any major study since 1933 when Austin Warren aimed at a similar comprehensiveness in his discussion of Burke's "Mind and Art" in a two-part essay in the *Sewanee Review.* The more recent studies usually explore some aspect of his criticism, focus on his theory of language or rhetoric, or treat him exclusively as a philosopher. The most rewarding of these later studies is William H. Rueckert's *Kenneth Burke and the Drama of Human Relations* (Minneapolis, 1963). Rueckert delineates the development of Burke's final system of thought and critical analysis, "Dramatism." A perfectly Burkean definition of Dramatism may be found in Webster's *Third New International Dictionary of the English Language:* a "technique of analysis of language [incl. literature] and thought as basically modes of action rather than as means of conveying information."

Rueckert maps out the high road to Dramatism by "cutting through the underbrush" of what he, like many, considers irrelevant and irritating terminological rank growth—by partly purifying Burke, as he says. There is no need to duplicate this excellent book, although expository and critical remarks on Burke's system of thought will also be a part of this study. But here the emphasis will be on a problem suggested by Rueckert's approach: when the survey of the main route to Dramatism is completed, what happens to the gores, the small angular pieces of land along the surveyed line? Do they fall to the surveyor "free gratis for nothing," as Mark Twain puts it in the "Professor's Yarn" episode of *Life on the Mississippi*? Or are they left for squatters to come and pick?

In so verbal a thinker as Burke, who cultivates the methodology of the pun, terminological peculiarities and complexities are certainly more than mere stylistic vagaries. With him, verbal figures virtually merge with figures of thought. He proceeds, by preference, on the byways and roundabouts of the mind. He will "with assays of bias/By indirections find directions out." In his own words: he likes to radiate. Even if he criticizes a view, he is reluctant to abandon it.

Such a reflexively ironic turn of mind makes for much essential complexity which cannot be hacked away without intrinsic damage. Nor is such a mode of thinking strange in a writer and critic who is centrally concerned with the imaginative strand of a work —with that of its aspects which is symbolic or characteristic of its author's engrossments, even obsessions. All these complexities, as manifest in Burke's speculative procedure and, especially neatly, in his imaginative work, must be faced and dealt with—at the cost of following a contradictory argument now and then.

These considerations suggest four levels at which the argument of the present book will have to be carried on: (1) an analysis of Burke's fiction and poetry; (2) an exposition of his theoretical writings, with special emphasis on his literary criticism; (3) a critical assessment of these theories; and (4) an attempt at times to turn Burke's own methodology of symbolic exegesis upon himself. This last aspect—the analysis of strategy, of attitude, the emotional factor, occupational interest, engrossment (what Burke calls the "hidden imposthume") in his own writings—plays a particularly important part in the effort to discount the merely attitudinal and strategic elements and to move toward the objective statement. In this sense, the semantic principle of unequivocal meaning hovers about the edges of Dramatism as the transcendental ideal of Burke's philosophy, unattainable, as he sees it, and therefore unattempted by him.

The argument of this study moves forward on these four tracks, with no intention to keep them neatly apart nor to alternate among them in any schematic way. After a first chapter of general introduction, the over-all progression is roughly chronological, with each chapter devoted to one book or a group of closely related ones. For reasons of space, documentation of merely parallel and complementary passages has, as a rule, been omitted. To make up for this omission, I should like summarily to acknowledge my indebtedness to the total body of Burke reviewing, criticism, and scholarship.

There is, then, on the one hand, Kenneth Burke, this veritable one-man department: poet, novelist, critic, musicologist, psychologist, sociologist, semanticist, moralist, cryptologist, "Burkologist," with his voluminous, difficult, and profound work—on the other, the present monograph: certainly a lopsided Dramatistic alignment. To be sure, the attempt at total inclusiveness imposes limitations upon this study, the inevitable limitations of selectiveness, restrictions of the perspective, and the necessary confines imposed by the scope and purpose of the series in which it appears. In keeping with the over-all literary perspective, it was, therefore, necessary to be more selective in dealing with Burke's general writings and occasionally to resort to paraphrase and summary, whereas the area of his fiction, poetry, and literary theory and criticism is as far as possible explored by means of the critical-analytical ideal, quotation and explication. Within this frame, the aim is neither to extoll nor to condemn Burke, but rather to understand his work, within the context of Dramatism and, possibly, beyond.

The writing of this study in its present form would not have been possible without a Fellowship from the Commonwealth Fund. This book may serve as a partial expression of my gratitude to all the officers of the Foundation and my sponsors. I am also grateful to Professors R. W. B. Lewis, Norman Holmes Pearson, and René Wellek, of Yale University, for more than only a careful reading of parts of the manuscript and for comments and suggestions. Thanks are also due to the *Hudson Review* and the *Texas Quarterly* for making galley proofs of current essays available. Finally, I am obviously indebted to Mr. Burke himself for his *herzliche* reception, his free discussions, and other kindnesses too numerous to specify. This personal relationship alone is a more than sufficient reward for the time and effort that went into the writing of this book.

ARMIN PAUL FRANK

Contents

Chronology

1897 Kenneth Duva Burke born May 5 in Pittsburgh, Pennsylvania.

1916 Attended Ohio State University for a semester.

1916–1917 Attended Columbia University; leaves a promising scholastic career to devote himself to writing.

1918 Lives in Greenwich Village. Burke, Malcolm Cowley, Matthew Josephson, Slater Brown, Hart Crane, Gorham B. Munson form an informal group of *avant-garde* writers.

1919 Marries Lillian Mary Batterham (three daughters).

1921 On the editorial board of *The Dial* where he continues, with brief intermissions, until the magazine ceases publication in July, 1929.

1922 Buys a farm near Andover, New Jersey, which he makes his permanent home.

1923 Temporarily co-editor of *Secession.* Much of his short fiction published.

1924 His short story, "Prince Llan," believed to be the cause of the suppression of *Broom* in January. A collection of short fiction, *The White Oxen,* and critical essays published.

1926–1927 Research worker, Laura Spelman Rockefeller Memorial Foundation.

1927–1929 Music critic, *The Dial.*

1929 January, Dial Award for distinguished services to American letters.

1929 Editorial work for Bureau of Social Hygiene.

1931 *Counter-Statement,* a collection of critical essays.

1932 *Towards a Better Life,* a novel.

1933 After divorce, marries Elizabeth Batterham (two sons).

1933 November to January, 1936, music critic, *The Nation.*

1935 Guggenheim Fellowship.

1935 April, participates in the First American Writers' Congress; member of the Executive Committee. Burke never a member of the Communist party.
1935 *Permanence and Change: An Anatomy of Purpose.*
1937 Lecturer in criticism, New School of Social Research. Beginning of a career as University Lecturer; only the more important affiliations are cited below.
1937 *Attitudes toward History.*
1938 Summer, Lecturer, University of Chicago; again 1949–50.
1941 *The Philosophy of Literary Form,* collection of criticism.
1943–1961 With intermissions, professor of criticism, Bennington College, Vermont.
1945 *A Grammar of Motives.*
1946 Member, National Institute of Arts and Letters.
1949 Member, Princeton Institute for Advanced Studies.
1950 *A Rhetoric of Motives.*
1955 *Book of Moments,* a selection of poetry.
1957–1958 Fellow, Center for Advanced Study in the Behavioral Sciences.
1961 *The Rhetoric of Religion.*
1964–1965 Regents Professor, University of California at Santa Barbara.
1966 July, Ph.D. (honorary), Bennington College. Rockefeller Grant. *Language as Symbolic Action: Essays on Life, Literature, and Method.*
1967 Member, American Academy of Arts and Sciences. Brandeis University Special Award for Notable Achievement in the Arts.
1967–1968 Winter, Lecturer, Harvard University.
1968 *Collected Poems: 1915–1967; The Complete White Oxen: Collected Short Fiction of Kenneth Burke.*

Kenneth Burke

CHAPTER 1

Curriculum Criticum

I *Young Man with a Propensity for Words*

WHAT am I but a *word man*"—thus, it is reported, Kenneth Burke once informally described himself to his friends.[1] This statement has become the defensively defiant motto of his life's work, culminating in his definition of man as the "symbol-using animal," no more, no less.[2] Although Matthew Josephson does not specify when Burke originally referred to himself in these terms, the context indicates that it was shortly after he quit college to devote himself to imaginative, critical, and speculative writing. He already had a number of published poems to his credit, most of them in *The Sansculotte,* an undergraduate magazine of Ohio State University at Columbus, where he had studied for one semester. There, Ludwig Lewisohn had guided him to the study of Thomas Mann's work, which became one of the models of Burke's own fiction.[3] In Mann's writings, he encountered, in artistic, eloquent form, elements of Nietzschean thought, which had made decisive contributions to the temper of the period. Friedrich Nietzsche and especially his disciple, the historian Oswald Spengler, were to exert a great influence on Burke's own work.

At least equally intensive is the effect which another important area of his early reading had on the formation of Burke's mind: nineteenth-century French literature, which he read extensively. It goes almost without saying that a literary-minded young man at that time virtually devoured the Symbolist poets and became an adept of the esthetes and "decadents" of that period. Burke published a Baudelairean prose poem in French; his first essay to be published was about Jules Laforgue. Among novelists, Gustave Flaubert impressed him most; but he became also engrossed with the work of J. K. Huysmans and other neo-Catholics; and he learned much from Remy de Gourmont and others who in their thought embraced the form, but not the content, of Catholic theology. These predilections led him to an early and lasting occupation with patristic and scholastic thought.

Even earlier, during his high school days, Burke had been in the literary crowd. As Malcolm Cowley, his earliest and closest friend, relates in his account of their common fledgling years, their reading of Oscar Wilde, G. B. Shaw, and the *Smart Set* had led them to consider the cult of the paradox, the outwitting of an audience, as the last word in modernism. Among their other early reading of English authors, of Rudyard Kipling, R. L. Stevenson, George Meredith, Thomas Hardy (and, especially for Burke, the euphuistic stylist, Walter Pater), Cowley singles out G. R. Gissing, in whose imaginary journal of a literary recluse, *The Private Papers of Henry Ryecroft* (1903), the boys found an opinion with which they agreed wholeheartedly: "I have never learned to regard myself as a 'member of society.' For me, there have always been two entities—myself and the world—and the normal relation between the two has been hostile." [4]

This view, which corresponded to their introverted sensitivity, was intensified by the problems of adolescence. It prepared Burke for the understanding of Mann who artistically encompassed this rift between man and society. And for the aspiring writers in the United States of that period, the expression of this conflict was charged with the intensity of immediate experience. It summed up what serious artists frequently had experienced as the over-all crass materialism, the Philistinism, and the provincialism of the country. It was partly this impression of a blighted cultural scene —variously expressed in such seminal works as Henry Adams' *Education* (1907) and Jack London's *Martin Eden* (1909)—which had made a literary exile of Henry James; which sent Gertrude Stein, Ezra Pound, and T. S. Eliot to Europe; and which continued to send to the Continent writers like Ernest Hemingway, E. E. Cummings, Cowley, Josephson, and many others.

II *A Literary Expatriate in His Own Country*

Kenneth Burke never went abroad, although in 1918 he cast his lot with the *littérateurs* and free lances and left Columbia University for Greenwich Village, where he lodged with another high school friend, James Light, the later director of some of O'Neill's plays; subsisting on ascetic rations, he was eager to complete and publish short stories and essays while his meager funds lasted. With Cowley, Josephson, Slater Brown, Hart Crane, and later Allen Tate, Robert Coates, J. B. Wheelwright, and G. B. Munson, he was a member of an informal group of literary avantgardists—individualists all, every member entertaining reservations concerning some opinion of every other, each one anxious to define his identity, anxious to write.

Cowley had already made his way to Europe to participate in World War I; others were to follow later in order to shop around with the Futurists and their aggressive technological optimism or with the Surrealists and their psycho-literary experiments; occasionally, they had a hand in the partial transformation of the latter movement into the radically anti-intellectual and aggressively anti-bourgeois convulsions of Dadaism; they witnessed the misery of the inflation that rocked the economy of most European countries; and they stayed just long enough to catch a glimpse of the political radicalism that was the outgrowth of all this turmoil. The writings that came of these assorted experiences went mostly into more or less short-lived little magazines, in the case of Burke's group primarily into *Broom* and *Secession* (whose co-editor Burke was in 1923), and in part into the *Literary Review* of the New York *Evening Post*. Burke shared vicariously in the European experiences of his friends owing to his, and their, epistolary diligence.

At the same time, disillusionment also increased in the United States. When military victory was won in 1918, the defeat which Woodrow Wilson's peace policy suffered at the hands of unrelenting European allies aided by an unscrupulous internal opposition was a serious setback. Under the slogan of "normalcy," the political and economic life of the United States turned back into another spell of isolationism and favored the single-minded pursuit of prosperity which characterized so much of the 1920's and led up—or down—to the big crash that terminated the decade. The general effects and consequences of this primarily economic development reinforced the twisted outgrowths of wartime patriotism which, on the fringe and beyond, led to quite solid manifestations of jingoism, racism, increasing Ku Klux Klan activities, and other forms of right-wing radicalism.

SAINT PETER'S COLLEGE LIBRARY
JERSEY CITY, NEW JERSEY 07306

The intellectual and cultural counteraction was intensive but restricted and not very effective. It was mainly characterized by the kind of holistic utopianism that William Wasserstrom somewhat dithyrambically treated as "organicism" in *The Time of the Dial.*[5] It had taken such forms as Randolph Bourne's "transnationality" and Alfred Stieglitz' idea of an integral society corresponding to the mind-body organism. These and related tendencies have their place in a strong American tradition of thought which goes back to such conciliators of evolutionary biologism and ethical philosophy as Chauncey Wright and John Fiske, and beyond that to Walt Whitman's view of the world as a dynamic revolutionary organism and Ralph Waldo Emerson's transcendentalist vision of the world as a universal poem. These ideas have their source in Coleridgean and German Romanticism.

At the other end, this trail leads into Burke's vision of the world in the light of the poetic metaphor, grounded upon the rock-bottom of man's universal biological nature which in the 1930's Burke sees as naturally ethical because, as a very organism, man must make choices; "all living things are critics," he says in *Permanence and Change.*[6] A conciliator of the 1920's and 1930's had, of course, to cope with a much wider range of disparate materials than his nineteenth-century predecessors—various schools of psychoanalysis, behaviorism, biological evolutionism, neurological researches, anthropological findings, social stirrings, Marxist determinism, and so on. Yet such a synthesis is exactly what Burke attempted.

III The Dial*'s Critic*

A publication that sponsored an integrative view of at least the arts had been Stieglitz' *The Seven Arts* (1916–17), and another, more cosmopolitan one in the 1920's was *The Dial* under the joint ownership of Scofield Thayer and J. S. Watson.[7] After April, 1925, the magazine was also shaped by the taste of Marianne Moore, who then became acting editor. Burke, who had begun to work for the *Dial* in 1921, continued on its editorial board in various capacities and with occasional intermissions until the magazine ceased publication in July, 1929. During the absence of Thayer and Gilbert Seldes in 1923, he was for several months in charge of editorial work, with Dr. Watson as final authority; starting in December, 1927, he became its music critic.

Many of Burke's early stories and seminal essays appeared in this magazine, which also serialized the first six chapters of his novel, *Towards a Better Life*. His criticism helped to shape the *Dial's* editorial policy, just as the exchange of views among the staff contributed to the rounding out of his own literary theory: more than ten years later, Burke dedicated *The Philosophy of Literary Form* (1941) to Watson. More immediately, and apart from several important translations both from the German and the French, three books came out of Burke's time with the *Dial: The White Oxen and Other Stories* (1924); *Counter-Statement* (1931), a collection of critical essays marking the first, formalist stage of his literary theory; and *Towards a Better Life, Being a Series of Epistles, or Declamations* (1932). Burke's achievement both as a critic and an imaginative writer was publicly recognized by the bestowal of the Dial Award for 1928, a distinction which had previously been conferred upon Sherwood Anderson, T. S. Eliot, Van Wyck Brooks, Marianne Moore, William Carlos Williams, and Ezra Pound.

The *Dial* board was the group to which Burke felt, and continues to feel, allegiance, especially as regards Miss Moore and Dr. Watson. When the review was discontinued shortly before the stock market collapse of 1929, an important factor in American cultural life ceased to exist; and the decisive formative phase of Burke's career came to a close. An interim occupation was his research on drug addiction which he did under Colonel Arthur Woods of the Rockefeller Foundation. This work equipped Burke for his own later studies of Coleridge. But as the Depression continued and deepened, he lost support also in a fundamentally existential sense. True, he could always come home to his New Jersey farm which he had bought in 1922, mostly from translator's fees and income from his other writings, and which had the necessary equipment for a self-reliant Thoreauvian mode of life—with one notable addition: Burke's family.

But for Burke, as for many other writers of that critical period, the Walden stance was no longer possible. To be sure, the earlier anti-societal estheticism—whether of the "Aesthete: Model 1924" or 1925 (or, for that matter, 1917) variety—had already been a kind of *group* attitude.[8] Yet now it was even more vital to "belong," to find one's self by identifying with a common cause. The economic plight with all its concomitant illnesses of the social body naturally and justly gave direction to the element of opposition contained in the earlier estheticism, and a small but militant group of international Communists was at hand to exploit this situation all the more easily because of the rise to power of fascism and nazism abroad and the increase of right-wing agitation at home.

IV *The Committed Decade*

Many intellectuals and writers certainly moved left at this time, although the incentive for this step frequently was not any political dogmatism at all; it sprang, instead, from humanistic and humanitarian motives. At any rate, Burke's type of communism was of an idealist, even Romantic cast; and it contained such disparate elements as agrarianism and bohemianism—a combination of almost Dadaist paradoxicalness. It is, therefore, not surprising that his books and other expressions of opinion encountered the pronounced disapproval of the Communist orthodoxy. (Yet, to be sure, criticism came from other quarters as well.)

Thus, for instance, "Revolutionary Symbolism in America," his contribution to the First American Writers' Congress held in New York City in April, 1935, aroused the solid indignation of many hard-core partisans. It was the most controversial paper of all and the most forward-looking (or most controversial *because* most forward-looking?).[9] Despite this criticism, however, Burke, who was among those who had signed the call for the congress, was elected a member of the Executive Committee of the newly founded League of American Writers. This organization was set up strictly according to Stalinist lines of regimentation—elections amounting to acclamations, since no alternative candidates were nominated, and vacancies in the various boards at the different hierarchic levels to be filled by appointment. This perfect method of controlling dissident members frequently amounted to controlling them out of the ranks.

Burke still read a paper at the second Writers' Congress in 1937—the list of his fellow speakers included such notables as Ernest Hemingway and Archibald MacLeish—but he no longer held any office. At the third congress, Burke reported about Hitler's *Battle;* but his anti-nazism now certainly transcended any shade of party communism. Such events as the Stalinist purges culminating in the spectacular Moscow trials of 1936–38, the Soviet Russian participation in the attack upon Poland initiated by Nazi Germany, and the Russian invasion of Finland in the fall of 1939 were eye-openers for many American Communist sympathizers. Burke remained an anti-Fascist, Agrarian liberal; but he became independent of any political affiliation and began to devote his time and energies to the expansion and elaboration of his coherent world view of Dramatism and to an activity that was completely new to him: university teaching.

V *Lecturer and Man of Letters*

Burke began his teaching career as a lecturer in criticism at the New School of Social Research in New York in 1937. The following summer, and later again in 1949–50, he taught at the University of Chicago. His first stay there coincided with the formative period of the Chicago School of Criticism. The book which took its final shape during this time is *The Philosophy of Literary Form,* which appeared in the same year as John Crowe Ransom's *The New Criticism* (1941); a reviewer aptly remarked that in view of *newness* the titles of the two books actually should have been interchanged.[10] *The Philosophy of Literary Form,* marking the middle phase of Burke's criticism, establishes him as a critic somewhat apart from the mainstream of the so-called New Criticism; the briefest way of characterizing his critical position in a single formula is to say that, similar to I. A. Richards, he is primarily concerned with the semantics and psychology of literature, with overtones of special anthropological and sociological concerns, plus a dose of pragmatism.

With the development of this seminal theory of literature, Burke returned to the field in which he is most competent, literary criticism, bringing to bear on it his knowledge of an extraordinarily wide range of diverse scientific disciplines which he had synthesized in the previous decade. The cornerstone of this enterprise is *Permanence and Change: An Anatomy of Purpose* (1935), Burke's "Vision"; *Attitudes toward History* (1937) is an important companion piece. After the codification of his revised literary theory in the *Philosophy of Literary Form,* Burke set out on another field trip into human knowledge—this time more in the area of formal philosophy, rhetoric, and theology—to return with the detailed map of his Dramatistic empire, delineated in *A Grammar of Motives* (1945), *A Rhetoric of Motives* (1950, again dedicated to Watson, this time under his pseudonym, W. C. Blum), and its logological offshoot, *The Rhetoric of Religion: Studies in Logology* (1961). The most recent collection of essays, *Language as Symbolic Action: Essays on Life, Literature, and Method* (1966—dedicated to "J. Sibling W[atson]") rounds out this *Motivorum Corpus* in the areas of psychology, linguistic theory, and literary criticism in the narrower sense. *Book of Moments* (1955) is a selection of the poetry which Burke wrote over the years. The *Collected Poems: 1915–1967* and *The Complete White Oxen: Collected Short Fiction of Kenneth Burke* appeared in 1968.

During all these years of work on his system of Dramatism, Burke held a teaching position at Bennington College, Vermont (1943–61). He also taught summer courses at Kenyon College in 1950, and elsewhere. After 1961, he was affiliated with Drew University, Pennsylvania State, the University of California at Santa Barbara, and Harvard University, in turn. He is a member of the National Institute of Arts and Letters and the American Academy of Arts and Sciences.

Dramatism, as developed by Burke, is a consistent world view. It is unique insofar as it takes ritual drama, or sacrificial tragedy, as the representative anecdote, or key example, of all human behavior—psychological, linguistic, social. It emerges in Burke's theory of the history of the West as a five-act drama (in *Attitudes toward History*) and is elaborated in *The Philosophy of Literary Form* as an ideal approach to both poetry and the social sciences. Critics have repeatedly said that Burke stopped being a good literary critic when he turned his attention to extra-literary concerns. He certainly never was exclusively an explicator of texts, though his analyses are always acute and stimulating. A great deal of his interests and energies has always been lodged in the theory of literature, the philosophy of language, and the contemplation of life.

On the other hand, it could in all fairness be said that Burke has come to a stop, a stop, however, not of failure but of achievement: he has no intention of going beyond Dramatism and logology, but he is constantly at work elaborating, subtilizing, and perfecting his position. Thus, for instance, *Language as Symbolic Action* presents, among other concerns, the latest stage of his Dramatistic criticism both in theory and in a far-ranging application to individual works. Burke's quest for *identity* has long come to a close; now, the Dark Tower's name is *consummation.*

CHAPTER 2

In Quest of Parnassus

AT the end of the title story of *The White Oxen* it is night, and Matthew Carr looks down over the Ohio River Valley.[1] For a few moments, his view of the rows of lights and tongues of flames that indicate the steel mills is transformed into a vision of promise, of hope, of futurity. Yet this elation soon passes and leaves him weakened, distressed, yearning for dullness, for the "blissful sloth of semi-sensation." About seven years or 231 pages later, toward the end of the last story, Prince Llan in a trance forces open a door and collapses over the grotesquely dismembered duplicate of his own body; dissolving into a gelatinous mass and dying, he pushes open another door, only to see one more corridor with still another closed door at the end. The essential similarity between these two moments is evident; but so is their difference, even if they are compared in isolation. Considered, however, within their proper narrative contexts in terms also of style and technique, these two incidents may well serve as indicators both of the progressive structure of *The White Oxen* and of its author's development as an imaginative writer. The exploration of this progression is the main concern of this chapter.

I *The Progressive Form of* The White Oxen

Between 1920 and 1924 the fifteen stories collected in *The White Oxen* had with one exception appeared in *Broom, The Dial, The Little Review, Manuscripts, S4N,* and *Secession.* The book contains almost the whole of Burke's published short fiction, although for reasons presently to be discussed, several of his other pieces merge fictional with essayistic or lyrical elements and constitute forms that oscillate between the stream-of-consciousness story, the introspective essay, and the *poème en prose.*

In the arrangement of *The White Oxen,* which roughly parallels the original publication of the different stories in the literary magazines, the whole displays a progression of method which the author interpreted as a "gradual shifting of stress away from the realistically convincing and true to life" to "a corresponding increase of stress upon the more rhetorical properties of letters" (WO, ix). Yet reviewers have argued that the stories which constitute the final stages of this development, far from communicating, actually keep their readers baffled; and therefore some of the critics have offered alternative interpretations of this progression: "from a reasonable clarity of vision, through progressive disintegration to an ultimate bogging down in an anarchy of metaphysics" (C. Hartley Grattan);[2] from social realism to romantic, heroic, cerebral, or dialectical fantasy, in turn (Matthew Josephson);[3] from subject matter to technique and form, that is, toward the abstract (Gorham B. Munson);[4] and from realism to "accuratism," a method which emphasizes the exact detail, but not for the purpose of a Naturalistic imitation (Malcolm Cowley).[5] And, as though to put an end to this apparent confusion, Austin Warren has offered a static interpretation of the book.[6]

Many of the commendatory as well as the few negative reviews agree, however, that, with the last story of *The White Oxen,* a cycle in the author's development has irrevocably come to a close; *where will Kenneth Burke go from here?* is a question in which more than one review culminates. The present analysis proposes to answer this question by exploring the exact nature of the methodical progression of *The White Oxen* and by pointing out its logical coherence with Burke's subsequent works. The thesis is that all the alternative interpretations, plus Burke's own view of the pattern of the book, can be subsumed under one heading because each of them contains a valid aspect; but none of them more than adumbrates the governing structural principle. Some theoretical considerations utilizing key concepts from Burke's criticism help to approach a solution; the final proof has, of course, to rely upon a reading of the relevant passages and stories.

The most appropriate point of departure is Burke's own concept of rhetoric. According to an important essay published shortly after *The White Oxen* and entitled "Psychology and Form,"[7] rhetoric is the exploitation of audience psychology. This definition can hardly be regarded as unorthodox; yet the conclusions to which it is pushed in this essay and in related sections of

Counter-Statement yield striking insights into the nature of literary appeal in general and into the functioning of Burke's fiction in particular. Accordingly, the procedure of rhetoric is the playing upon universally shared appetites for psychic involvement: the audience, Burke says, likes to be engrossed by the pleasurable pattern of raising and satisfying expectations; and Burke's personal taste prefers this pattern of suspense and revelation to operate not so much through the gross structure of the plot as through the sentence by sentence and word by word texture—through eloquence.

This emphasis on the "microscopic" aspects of movement in an imaginative work is bound to minimize factual detail, subject matter, hero psychology, the "realism" of setting and plot. In other words (to use a spatial metaphor), conventional realistic fiction can always be analyzed as a two-level structure consisting of an exterior and an interior action, the physical action and the hero (or character) psychology. The narrator's point of view serves as a linking as well as complicating factor. But, underneath this structure, there is a third strand: that of the expressive act, or composition, which serves as the principle of unity governing all details of the other two.

To be sure, in realistic stories this underlying level of motivation is in turn determined by the exigencies of a realistic plot. But, in the later *White Oxen* stories, the underlying "symbolic action" (as Burke later calls this principle of unity in *The Philosophy of Literary Form*) rises to the surface, fully asserts itself: it rejects the restrictions imposed by the superstructure and conjoins story elements such as vignettes (rudimentary episodes), glimpses of character, isolated images, perspectives, postures, and the like, in such a way as to form narrative patterns that are immediately and almost exclusively controlled by this underlying act. Because of this dominating role of the expressive element, fiction of this kind appears as a meditative and confessional genre: as the verbalization of the poet's burden. To the extent, however, that such stories are not merely introspective jottings—that they originate in the interaction of "creative germs" with an artistic mastery of language, as do most of Burke's stories of this type—they are also communicative. This rhetorical quality is intensified by the fact that these stories minimize the interest in the kind of eventfulness which a plot provides and feature the interest in stylistic expression.

These considerations suggest a general frame of reference for describing the progression of the *White Oxen* stories. The sequence can conveniently be broken down into three fairly coherent groups of stories which may pragmatically—and provisionally, as far as the last group is concerned—be labeled: (1) the early stories of symbolic realism; (2) various types of dramatic monologues and related forms; and (3) surrealistic fables.

II *The Early Stories*

The first and most clearly defined group consists of the title story, of "The Excursion," "Mrs. Maecenas," and "Olympians." With the possible exception of "The Excursion," these stories are recognizably set in a world that is encompassed by the horizon of (Pittsburgh, Pennsylvania) lower-middle-class people, a Midwestern college, and suburbia. They are studies in the psychology of alienation, the dominant theme being the frustration of the adolescent as he gradually faces the complexities of life. The theme as such is somewhat reminiscent of Sherwood Anderson and of the early Hemingway; so is the groping expressionism manifest in the occasionally strained manipulations of some of the symbols.

In contradistinction to Anderson's and Hemingway's fiction, however, Burke's tyro usually moves in some part of the universe of arts and letters, however modest. Siegfried, for instance, in "Mrs. Maecenas," is a superb study of an undergraduate intellectual in a small Midwestern college. The same type had once before played an incidental yet characteristic part in "The White Oxen," a remarkably well-executed novelette *à la* Flaubert, in which the social contacts of a simple but not insensitive adolescent are focused and intensified by his symbolically recurrent encounters with a herd of white oxen at the zoo. On the whole, these early stories are characteristic of the young author's mastery of the conventional style of symbolic realism. The descriptive material is artfully selected and exact; the images are poignant and functional. Both these elements vie with shrewdly manipulated cliché phrases to produce a tone of *impassabilité* (or detachment, a tone that betrays no emotional involvement on the part of the narrator with his characters and their actions)[8] and mild irony toward the unfolding situation. Only occasionally does the irony overreach itself to mar the tone with a note of *Smart Set* smartness.

"Olympians" stands somewhat apart from the other stories in this group. In the first place, the central personage is an elderly gentleman confronted with an additional twist of life's complexities. An artistically minded but weak character, Mr. Beck has never quite come to grips with life. He spends his days as a private music instructor in Edgewood, an all-American community. Given a situation like this, cultural criticism is an almost inevitable ingredient; its tone, that of gentle satire, is in perfect keeping with the over-all mode of presentation—symbolic realism. The important distinctive trait of this story, however, is a structural element, the treatment of the culminating symbol. The particular mode of its use introduces a poetic dimension that had been absent from the earlier *White Oxen* stories and, as such, marks the end of the first stage of development.

Mr. Beck, the meek and mildly frustrated introvert, is an American cousin of the outsiders and odd originals of Thomas Mann's fiction. Similar to Detlev Spinell in Mann's "Tristan," he is a "compleat" although slightly morose gentleman whose sensibility remains inarticulate beneath the veneer of a modest yet absorbing occupation in which he, however, excels in his gentle ways. Owing to his cardiac rheumatism, he is "denied vigorous exertion" and takes music as an anodyne. Although universally liked as a lecturer at local cultural events, although an "asset to the community," he is not really "in." His diffidence and his personal predicaments had the result that "Mr. Beck was sweetly and inexorably removed from the class of eligible men, and looked upon as a kindly institution. With an unquestioning docility, he walked in the path that was laid out for him, shielded his failing soul with umbrella and galoshes, kept it sufficiently warm with the horrible respect of his acquaintances" (WO, 99).

An admirable balance of pointed yet never aggressive satire and subtly shifting point of view sustains the whole story. The crisis is reached when middle-aged Mr. Beck begins to feel an infatuation for his "favourite pupil" Dorothy, when, one spring, the "Olympian was rising within him. . . . Apollo was stirring; balder . . ." (WO, 101). Of course, the fifteen-year-old girl remains unresponsive to his slight if humiliating attempts at courtship; she does, in fact, not even understand them. All that is left for him is to "annihilate Dorothy from his head." His solution is completely in keeping with his pathetic character: he takes her to an opera; and, afterwards fusing his own predicament with the memory of the event, he attains both a substitute gratification and a transference. On their way home, the streetcar "passed dark houses, shutting away all manner of things; houses that stood out frankly and openly, but within their walls, what slinking possibilities; houses with black corridors, with furniture and people in the shadows. These were sleeping houses, and as secret as caves" (WO, 104).

This closing passage is a clear indicator of the turn the progression of *The White Oxen* is taking. The dark houses are evidently a symbol, an objectivation of the hero's state of mind. The similarity with the symbolic use of the herd of white oxen in the title story is obvious; yet the symbolic houses, as used here, have an additional quality. Whereas in the earlier stories a descriptive detail could become symbolic by force of repetition and insistence, in "Olympians" a kind of intrinsic relation between sign and signified object establishes symbolism at the very first occurrence:[9] the dark, silent houses, secret as caves, full of slinking possibilities, immediately suggest "internality," psychic processes, and a troubled state of mind, just as the emphasis on depth, cavities, secret passageways, and aimless wandering in Burke's later story, "The Book of Yul," gives the impression of an immediate sensual depiction of deep-down ruminations.

Related instances of the same scene-act ratio[10] frequently occur in literature. One need only recall the ghostly vistas and flights of obscured rooms in the mansion in "The Jolly Corner," James's introspective fable of a quest for identity, or the description of the interior of the complex dormitory in Poe's fable of haunted conscience, "William Wilson": "But the house! . . . There was really no end to its windings—to its incomprehensible subdivisions. It was difficult, at any given time, to say with certainty upon which of its two stories one happened to be. . . . Then the lateral branches were innumerable—inconceivable—and so returning in upon themselves, that our most exact ideas in regard to the whole mansion were not very far from those with which we pondered upon infinity." [11]

It should go without saying that these comparative remarks are not in any way intended as entries in a universal dictionary of symbols in literature. Only in a quite specific context, and only when certain characteristic traits are present, is it admissible to consider houses and towns in a literary work as symbols of psychic processes. Yet one should not overlook this possibility when the conditions are fulfilled. In "Olympians," the whole development of the plot prepares for this kind of symbolic interpretation of the dark, silent houses. And, as such a symbol of internality (psychic life), the houses, over and above their function within the story, serve as a signal for a change in narrative method. They mark the end of the realistic period of Burke as an imaginative writer. Just as in this image the hidden workings of the mind become symbolically palpable to the senses, in the later *White Oxen* stories the underlying symbolic action more and more asserts itself as the surface principle of organization.

III *The Middle Phase*

The second group, then, gradated within itself, consists of the stories "Scherzando," "Portrait of an Arrived Critic," "David Wassermann," "After Hours," "My Dear Mrs. Wurtelbach," and "The Death of Tragedy." The scene has changed from the town to a megalopolis, sometimes recognizable as New York City. The stories are mostly set among Bohemians and artists, among young *littérateurs* wrestling with the facts of their flesh and blood and mind, with metaphysics and esthetics, and with society. The themes, too, become more complex. The basic lineup is still the artistically minded individual against society, but the theme oscillates in many-faceted refractions. Bitter irony predominates. David Wassermann, for instance, is faced with the choice of becoming a disinherited *avant-garde* artist or, casting his lot with capitalism, the junior partner in his father's "Greater New York Clothing Company, a growing organization, you see" (WO, 145). His final acceptance of the business proposition is presented as a defeat; but the alternative "success" of his writer-friend also ends in frustration.

The radical/reactionary conflict is carried into the community of letters itself. In "Portrait," the literary figure, Alfred, the arrived critic and gentleman, is the butt of the complex satire. Clearly, the satirical element is on the increase and extends from cultural to social criticism, notably in "Mrs. Wurtelbach" and in the first part of "Death" which, next to some of E. E. Cummings' poems, contains some of the most articulate and compact literary indictments of "healthy Americanism." The pattern of values at cross-purposes is additionally complicated by the theme of the ambiguity of progress which, together with the rebuff to realism, inspires the grotesque image of the artificial hippopotamus that dominates the coda of the transitional piece, "Scherzando." Technological progress is set off against natural beauty which, in the city, can only be a matter of memory. And, indeed, some of the memorable passages in these stories are vistas of scenic beauty recollected in the hurry and bustle of city life:

> On the other hand, oh, God, on the other hand, we shall sail easily across an enthusiasm of contours. To the south, the broad back of a hill curved down slowly into the plateau. And still farther south, an opposing curve swelled up and stretched away in the haze. While the lake fitted itself silently into the basin which the glaciers had scooped out for it some thousands of years ago. . . . Or trees banked up the mountain-side like clouds, and at irregular intervals the black-green firs jutting out like a city of church spires. (WO, 187–88)

Along with the new thematic complexity and the new locale, new techniques are introduced: types and combinations of stream-of-consciousness narrative, *style indirect libre,* dramatic monologues, declamations, harangues. Like Gulliver, the narrator frequently is nothing but a recording eye; unlike Gulliver, however, he often observes himself participate, or almost observes himself observe—strange modes of literary schizophrenia which are sometimes, as in "After Hours," naturalistically motivated by alcoholic excesses. In many instances, the narrator figure is a more or less clearly recognizable mask of the author: most obviously, perhaps, the Howard who figures prominently in "After Hours" and, incidentally, in "Death." The resemblances with Swift's writings are indeed remarkable: the same bitter understatement, the same olfactory misanthropy, even the coincidence of little details. The most striking similarity, as Malcolm Cowley correctly observes, is the acute personal feeling of the unclean and the clean that Swift and Burke, judged by their writings, seem to share.[12]

IV *The End of the Progression*

The third group of stories in *The White Oxen* is introduced by an introspective nightmare with parabolic overtones, "The Book of Yul," and consists of different kinds of fables: "A Progression," whose very structure imitates the leading up toward a moral fairy tale; "In Quest of Olympus," a surrealistic parable of adolescence; "First Pastoral," a straightforward legendary tale of spiritual distress, of an acute conflict between spirituality and sensuality; and finally "Prince Llan," which is built around a similar conflict, that of man as lover and man as thinker, and which tries to explore the possibility of their reconciliation in an antinomian "dualism not of strife but of mutual completions" (WO, 294), of reaching the salvation of quietude by going through the passional stage. Its ending, however, is a most emphatic assertion of finality—or is it futility? Both main figures die, the tutor, Gudruff, and the searcher, Prince Llan. There is the concluding vista of the closed door at the end of the corridor. In a coda, the fictional author addresses himself to the audience and announces enigmatically that he has just taken poison: "Ivn, you are dying! Not an aggregate of units, not a relative trifle in the light of Jupiter, but you, I—I— . . . I am dead./(Dies.)" (WO, 297).

As far as technique is concerned, "Llan" resembles "Quest" very closely; and, since the earlier story is not so fraught with philosophy and meditation, it is more easily amenable to a closer analysis of the technique of Burke's fiction of this phase. On the surface, "Quest" is a jumble of unrelated and fantastically disparate incidents. A hallucinatory quality permeates all parts, even the most naturalistic ones. Formally, the story is divided into five numbered sections. The action is set in (1) a subterranean cave, (2) a rural area, (3) a Walhalla-like heaven, (4) West Sixteenth Street, New York City, and (5) another heaven and later New York City and vicinity. The structural demarcations of the narrative, however, cut across these external, formal subdivisions: there are four narrative units, or episodes.

In the first episode, a first-person narrator drifts in a boat on a subterranean lake; he manages to escape by climbing through a narrow funnel high overhead which leads him into a rural area full of brambles and bushes. He recognizes that this place is "where Treep used to live." Here, in the middle of the first formal section, the story shifts to the second episode, a third-person narrative of the adventures of said Treep: on the behest of his master, Treep had felled a huge oak; killed by the falling tree, he became magnified and literally climbed into heaven, where he battled and vanquished an evil god, Arjk, and assumed his name. He became a loyal follower of the supreme godhead of this heaven, Wawl, until he in turn was vanquished by the Blizzard God whom he had tried to stop from pursuing Hyelva, a goddess. Ravaging her, the Blizzard God tore her white garments which fell down upon Earth as snow.

This episode carries the narration through the latter half of the first section up to the end of the third. At this point it metaphorically follows the falling snow to another—though thwarted—seduction scene in the lowly setting of New York's Bohemia. Alcohol-inspired disputations and the composition of a mediocre poem conclude this episode which, for once, coincides with a formal subdivision. In the final section, a first-person narrator, taking the cue from the invocation of the Trinity in the last stanza of the poem, relates his idea of its mode of existence—a sordid Laputan vision. The narrative then shifts to an outrageously ironic report of Christ's visit to New York City and the Phariseeism of his reception by the city administration. In the end, Jesus, meditating in a New Jersey cemetery, is met by the Heavenly Host and led back into heaven in the midst of "Seraphic Maneuvers," and accompanied by ecstatic stammerings: "Olammeth! . . . the seed/ . . . This sudden certainty!/Fulfillment, bursting through the mists/Olammeth, His Breasts!/Across night/Projected . . . (latent) . . . /when lo! the *Sun!*/Heaven's Gate swung shut" (WO, 255).

This summarizing paraphrase may possibly communicate the bewilderment one is likely to feel when first reading "Quest." For in this story, series of events distinctly separated by their modes of existence in time and space and in reflection are incongruously juxtaposed. The different narrative units are connected by qualitative progression and by repetition with variations—techniques which suggest musical forms of development. At the same time, they are associatively conjoined, in accordance, as it were, with the opening sentence: "With an uncertain tide . . . I simply took all chances and allowed myself to drift."

V *Collage as a Literary Technique*

Yet this association is only seemingly "free." A result of careful construction, it seems to resemble the radio and movie technique of montage. But in montage the coherence of the constituent elements (vignettes) is much more obvious than in the case of "Quest," where the individual narrative units lack both a common central personage and an immediately recognizable common theme. Furthermore, a montage, though not realistic in the strict sense of the word, usually has a realistic or near-realistic function as it achieves special effects of pacing, foreshortening, panoramic view, and so on. Nevertheless, a non-realistic element lurks about its edges and comes into its own when apparently incoherent vignettes are conjoined to a strictly non-realistic sequence, when montage becomes collage. In fact, the term "collage," which was originally used as a label for certain Cubist, Dadaist, and Surrealist pictorial techniques, does not only serve as an ideal tool for the analysis of "Quest" and other pieces of Burke's later fiction; as it will presently be shown, analogous concepts are also central to much of Burke's critical theory. These implications can be worked out by a short examination of the concept of collage in its artistic and ideological context. The emphasis here is on its relevance as a tool for analyzing imaginative literature; its importance for Burke's criticism will be more fully discussed in the proper context.

"Ce n'est pas la colle qui fait le collage," Max Ernst, the renowned Dadaist artist, writes in "La Mise sous Whisky Marin": it is not the glue that makes the collage.[13] Rather, collage is "the exploitation of the chance meeting of two distant realities on an unfamiliar plane or, to use a shorter term, the culture of systematic displacement and its effects." According to Ernst, the most important of these effects is the testing of an object's identity by means of a clashing juxaposition with another identity. To use this example: if two commonplace things, a canoe and a vacuum cleaner, are confronted with each other in a place where they are actually *out of place*, as in a forest, each of them "will pass from its false absolute, through a series of relative values, into a new absolute value, true and poetic: canoe and vacuum cleaner will make love." The underlying assumption is that "identity will be convulsive or will not exist."

In fact, this view of the discontinuity of existence and its corollary, the "complexity" of the individual, which Ernst shares with his fellow Dadaists and Surrealists, notably with André Breton, defines his place in a characteristic climate of ideas. The immediate ideological context, beyond that of Surrealism, is that of the Decadents and Symbolists of the *fin de siècle* and turn-of-the-century periods. A key role in the dissemination of this tradition is played by Remy de Gourmont, notably by his conception of the intellect as the storage place and exchange of opposing viewpoints. According to him, the intellect's supreme occupation is the "dissociation of ideas," ideas (impressions, mental images) which chance, emotion, pleasure, and interest have previously associated in conventional and arbitrary ways.[14] In English literature, Pound's concept of the Image as the instantaneous presentation of an intellectual and emotional complex, the superposition of what he calls two "ideas" (sense impressions or memories of such), has its place in the same tradition.[15] The one important scientific parallel is the development of psychoanalysis from applied hypnosis to a coherent view of man as an incoherent bundle of reflexes and complexes. Characteristically, the conception of man as manifest in *The White Oxen* has been described almost in identical terms.[16]

These remarks concerning the ideological background may suffice to put Ernst's artistic practice into the proper relief. In his collages, the most down-to-earth elements are conjoined to completely Surrealistic structures; irrationalism is achieved by completely rational methods. His materials are mostly lithographs and prints, but their composition attains the most brilliant effects of subconscious appeal, especially in his later collage novels such as *La Femme 100 Têtes* (1929) and *Une Semaine de Bonté* (1934). It is from this practice and from Ernst's theories that the term "collage" can most easily be borrowed as a tool of literary analysis.[17]

For Ernst has also shown an awareness of the literary aspect of the concept of collage by referring to "verbal collages" such as the title term of his treatise on collage, "*Whisky Marin*," an obvious transformation of "*aquamarin*," the color. In discussing Ernst's collages, Louis Aragon praises him for working by a process which is absolutely analogous to that of the poetic image and arriving at a completely homogeneous picture which is distinct from the purely plastic collages made by the earlier Cubists.[18] Ernst also explicitly refers to Rimbaud's speculations on hallucination and verbal alchemy,[19] thereby showing his awareness of a poetic tradition which had fully developed techniques of conjoining disparate material long before related methods and the name "collage" were developed in the representational arts.

In fact, Ernst's canoe-vacuum cleaner example is an immediate echo of Lautréamont's famous simile, "beau . . . comme la rencontre fortuite sur une table de dissection d'une machine à coudre et d'un parapluie." [20] This "convulsive" metaphor, characteristic of new impulses in nineteenth-century French poetry, in turn has its own long tradition which encompasses all those poetic moments in which violent metaphors play havoc with primal reality and propriety. It comes to the fore in a great deal of Symbolist poetry, in Rimbaud's tempestuous hallucinations, in Mallarmé's fragmentated compositions; later, in Apollinaire's Surrealistic compilations of cliché phrases and snippets of routine conversations, and in Eluard's gracefully distorted dreamlike invocations. Moreover, Pound's and Eliot's techniques of poetic quotation, particularly in those instances in which the allusive function of the quotation is minimal, belong in the same general tradition. The last instance differs from Burke's practice insofar as in his stories he does not use quoted material, although he sometimes does do so in his poems.

More recently, the collage of cliché phrases and beginners' instruction-manual speech has been adapted to theatrical diction, notably by Ionesco. There have also been some attempts at writing Cubist novels such as Gide's *Les Faux-monnayeurs* (1925). But collage experiments in the novelistic and dramatic genres are limited by the demands of the over-all structure. There, the realistic or near-realistic plot requirements of consistency and logical consequence hold their own against the collage principle of planned displacement, distortion, and inconsistency. As a consequence, collage in literature is most successful in poetry; in drama and fiction it usually remains restricted to the verbal level and manifests itself in such rhetorical devices as the *anacoluthon* (break in grammatical sequence) which, characteristically, is among the favored figures both in Burke's fiction and in his verse (WO, 187, 188; LSA, 322, etc.).[21]

Because of these difficulties intrinsic to the medium, collage in fiction works best in the short story where effects analogous to painted collage (Surrealist paintings) can be achieved. In such cases, fictional elements of the author's invention, not extraneous material, is compiled in ways which are fictionally incongruous; yet they cohere on a deeper level, as fantasies, dreams, subconscious projections.

VI *"In Quest of Olympus" as Literary Collage*

An analysis of Burke's story, "In Quest of Olympus," in terms of collage thus understood, reveals its structure by disclosing the unity of the underlying symbolic act. One of the literary means of achieving the abruptness and violence of collage juxtaposition in this story is the clash of formal and subject matter subdivisions. Another unmistakable collage element occurs in the middle of (formal) Section I at the place where the second narrative unit begins (cf. above, p. 37): "[Emerging from the underground cavity,] I was kept busy dodging beneath the low crooked branches, making detours, or creeping through chance holes in the foliage. And then of a sudden I broke through to a road, and looked across broad easy meadows . . . and why! there was the house where Treep used to live! And that stump in front of Treep's house, that was where the oak used to be which Treep had loved so much . . ." (WO, 253).

Narratively, a shift into the remote past occurs at this point. In terms of collage technique, however, this transition indicates that material of an earlier stylistic "origin" is superimposed upon more recent material, as when a figure from an old-style engraving or a print is pasted on a photograph. Characteristically, the locale of the second narrative unit is for the most part a kind of mythical Nordic heaven that is, indeed, very remote in time. In this sense, the transitional shift of tenses indicates a long lapse of time, but not necessarily into the past; the successional structure of the symbolic action underneath the disparity of fictional detail asserts itself. In keeping with this principle, the different heroes of the different narrative units are telescoped into one.

The basic unified progression of "Quest" now appears as follows: the story begins with a metaphoric representation of birth; the tree-cutting incident, after a long lapse of time, signifies the breaking loose from the familial bonds. The name Treep clearly is an indicator of the hero's familial alignment with the *tree*. In his criticism, Burke frequently refers to the tree as a symbol of (paternal) authority (PC, 71–72)[22]—nor should this be an overly eccentric notion. The command for rejecting the paternal rule is given by a "master" (or non-parental authority) and leads to the affiliation with even another authority, Wawl, the lord of the fictitious Nordic heaven. The mythical setting and tone of this episode and of the next adumbrate the still adolescent, immature character of the hero; so does the fact that he assumes the name and therefore identity of one of the most disliked gods.[23]

The next major incident is the gallant attempt to save a goddess from being raped. Not that such an undertaking is a common venture of young men, but it reflects certain adolescent attitudes toward the other sex. The exalted tone and mythical setting perfectly correspond with the emotional quality of such gallantry. The subsequent shift of tone and setting toward the squalid is the more fitting since the next phase of development involves the hero figure himself in an act of sexual aggression. Unsuccessful for the time being, the consummation occurs in the final section of the story. Prepared by a period of vituperation, black humor, Rabelaisian exuberance, and similar conflicting attitudes, the final ascension scene is undoubtedly orgasmic; even the cryptic meaning of "Heaven's Gate" has been explicitly prepared for earlier in the story.

In the light of this reading, "In Quest of Olympus" appears in close thematic relationship with the earlier initiation stories in *The White Oxen*. The title also connects it with "Olympians," where the term "Olympian" clearly has sexual overtones.[24] The pattern of the book, *The White Oxen,* thus appears as a clear and unified progression of technique, with a remarkably stable thematic core. The development is indeed away from Realism and directed toward Cubism and Surrealism. The term "collage," used in the analysis of the stories that constitute the terminal group of this progression, subsumes the different views of the previous reviewers: on the surface level, there is "disintegration," the displacement of elements—the "abstraction" from their "natural" contexts, whereas they are in themselves "accurately" presented. Such stories are "fantastic" as immediate projections of symbolic action; they are "rhetorical" in the sense that they speak to the audience more directly than would be feasible through a plot—in fact, the book culminates in an explicit address to the reader. In such structures, the element of meditation—"metaphysics"—overshadows plot—"myth" in the Aristotelian sense.

VII *Toward Further Developments*

Where will Burke go from here? An answer may be attempted by applying one of his own analytical techniques, the comparison of the first and last words and sentences of the book (CS, ix). Here, the progression is amazing: from "It is doubtful just what might have happened" to ". . . but I am dead./(Dies.)." The speaker who makes this announcement in the most emphatic accents of finality—"I am dead," not "I am dying"!—is the fictitious narrator of the last story who has just similarly dispensed with his hero. Has Burke's imaginative self died? There are strong extraneous indications that it has—almost. But consider the very last word: "Dies." Who is its speaker? A new self, reborn? The old self, doggedly persisting in its old ruts even after it has been decreed dead? At any rate, there is a near-catastrophe and a very narrow escape—by a single word!

The merger of the fictional with the essayistic in the collage stories foreshadows Burke's later development. Imaginatively, it leads toward the declamations or epistles of *Towards a Better Life;* discursively, toward the parallel quest for Permanence in Change, for *Attitudes toward History.* But, in the meantime, a critical voice speaks up to pronounce a remarkable *Counter-Statement.*

CHAPTER 3

Art as Anti-tude

I *The Key Example of Burke's Theory of Form*

THE key text for Burke's theory of form as developed in *Counter-Statement* is *Hamlet* Act I, Scene iv (CS, 29–30); and a short paraphrase of Burke's analysis of this scene may serve best as an introduction to a discussion of his early esthetic. The encounter of Hamlet with the ghost of his father, anticipated since the beginning of the play, does not occur until the fourth scene; and even then the confrontation is brought about by a series of accelerating and retarding moments. It is just past midnight; Hamlet, Horatio, and Marcellus, keeping guard on the parapet, expect the ghost to appear at any moment. Hardly has Horatio mentioned this fact, when, startlingly, there is "a flourish of trumpets, and two pieces go off"; this momentarily intensifies, but then diverts their (and the audience's) expectation. For this signal, as Hamlet explains, indicates only that the King's carousal is in full swing.

This episode is useful and effective in a number of ways. It not only distracts the attention; but, by evoking a contrasting scene of merriment, it also points up the loneliness of the three men and the secrecy of their endeavor. Furthermore, it suggests a topic of conversation: Hamlet begins to denounce the excessive drinking habits of his country, singling them out as the one point of offense which "in the general censure" constitutes the germ of the corruption of the Danes, a cause of "scandal." [1] At this moment, when the focus of interest apparently is off the subject, the ghost appears; and Hamlet addresses him in a resounding speech: "Angels and ministers of grace defend us!/Be thou a spirit of health or goblin damned. . . ."

Implicit in this "representative anecdote," as Burke later calls such a key example (GM, 59–61), are all permanent elements of his early critical theory. Accordingly, the incidents of a successful scene must be arranged so as to play upon the audience's expectations, raising them, directing them, then frustrating them temporarily, but finally gratifying them more fully by surprise and by an impressive speech, "a second burst of trumpets, perhaps even more effective than the first, since it is the rich fulfilment of a promise" (CS, 30). The *form* of the scene, then, corresponds to the *audience's* (not the hero's) *psychology.*

II *The Limited Perspective of This Analysis*

Communication, rhetoric, the work-audience ratio are indeed key issues in *Counter-Statement.* By at least temporarily limiting his critical considerations exclusively to these concerns, Burke was able to work out a number of important principles of formalist criticism which have not yet been superseded. The price for these insights gained by limiting the perspective (by a "trained incapacity," as—following Veblen—he was to call this technique in *Permanence and Change*) was later paid by Burke when it became necessary for him to "discount," to discuss "compensatory gains." For there are indeed important aspects of the scene from *Hamlet* which cannot be accounted for strictly in terms of form as audience psychology.

In fact, every single phase of this scene which plays upon the audience's expectations is also motivated in terms of the situation so far delineated in the play, so that form becomes just as much a function of subject matter as of audience psychology. For, when the general laws of *audience* psychology require a diversion, and Hamlet, motivated by the flourish of trumpets, begins to denounce Danish drinking habits, the choice of this *particular* topic is clearly determined by *hero* psychology: Hamlet acts in keeping with his hostile attitude toward the King and Queen as previously revealed in Act I, Scene ii. To be sure, this aspect of a work's structure receives attention later in the book, first in the parenthetic remark that "anything which made [a] delay possible without violating the consistency of the subject" is formally justified (CS, 33); then in a footnote which refers to hero psychology ("a certain kind of person") as a "static symbol" underlying the "dynamic one"—character determining the unfolding action (CS, 60n); and later this aspect is codified in general as "repetitive form" (CS, 125). But any such consideration is strikingly absent from the analysis of the representative anecdote and even later is not given much prominence.[2]

A second observation indicates even more precisely what elements are slighted in Burke's psychological formalism. Does the appearance of the ghost really come at such an unexpected time, when "scandal" is the cue? True, Hamlet's accusations divert the audience's attention, particularly since his speech is rhetorically complicated. But, beyond these superficial distractions, isn't a diatribe against the universal rottenness of Denmark the most appropriate preparation for the ghost's appearance, since he is both victim and symbol of the very same corruption? Isn't this a *thematic* coherence which adds more to the effect of the scene than the merely formal contrast of surprise? Again, this feature can be interpreted in terms of principles which Burke developed later; but he takes no note of it here.

Finally, the lofty rhetoric of Hamlet's speech when he addresses the ghost is rewarding not only because it has been delayed but perhaps even more so because it clearly and emphatically announces a new phase of thematic development, because it makes a new promise, raising as it does the problem of the ghost's nature —is he good or evil? The action thus embarks upon a new purpose, the discerning of the ghost. *Significance* supervenes the mere play upon the audience's emotions. A fuller analysis of the scene is therefore possible. Yet, within the compass of Burke's theory, a tool for such an analysis becomes available only at a much later stage, when the concept of the tragic rhythm of action is formulated in *A Grammar of Motives* (cf. below, Chapter 8, Section II b).

The critical theory of *Counter-Statement*, however, is not yet especially concerned with hero psychology, thematic coherence, and significance (or purposiveness). But these conscious or unconscious omissions have a strategic value insofar as they made it possible for Burke to formulate an excellent definition of literary form without incurring the danger of becoming narrowly formalistic. It would, in fact, have been impossible to devise such a theory without temporarily disregarding recalcitrant material. As a consequence, much of Burke's later critical theory is necessarily devoted to rounding out the position by making the requisite modifications. Yet the above considerations do bring home the fact that the most appropriate perspective for analyzing Burke's critical theory as of *Counter-Statement* is to focus on the dialectics of strategic limitation, of "trained incapacity." Equal emphasis may then be placed upon the virtue of limitation as the generative force of brilliant critical principles and upon its disadvantage, insofar as it requires complicated tactics for admitting the omissions as it were by the back door.

III *The Significance of* Counter-Statement

This dual rôle of limitation is reflected by the very nature of *Counter-Statement* as a collection of intimately interrelated essays which progressively amplify and correct one another. Containing essays that had previously appeared in literary magazines, as well as pieces published for the first time, the book is a representative selection of Burke's critical output during the 1920's to and including the year of publication, 1931. According to the preface, it "should serve to elucidate a point of view" (CS, viii), a "heretic" view, whose every single thesis and theory runs counter to a corresponding tenet of the critical orthodoxy of the time (CS, vii).

If one analyzes this point of view *synchronically* (statically), as William H. Rueckert does in *Kenneth Burke and the Drama of Human Relations,* one can distinguish three apparently contradictory ingredients in the esthetic of *Counter-Statement:* (1) It propounds a theory of pure art whose end is eloquence and exaltation; (2) it defends art as revelation, maintaining that the end of poetry is wisdom; and (3) it claims that art has a cathartic function. To reconcile these conflicting clauses, Rueckert singles out the "attitude of critical openness, the both/and doctrine" as the center of this critical theory.[3]

IV *The Essentially Antithetical Nature of Syncretism*

Although the second aspect as analyzed by Rueckert is considerably less prominent than the other two, and although a fourth clause, "art is the corrective of overly assertive society," should be complemented to round out such a static analysis of *Counter-Statement,* the featuring of *syncretism* as the core of Burke's critical attitude is certainly correct.[4] Syncretism, a stoical attitude that endeavors to balance and conciliate conflicting viewpoints, indeed underlies Burke's total philosophy: it aims at an undogmatic yet highly critical admission, entertaining, and working up of all possible conflicting doctrines.[5]

In terms of esthetic, this program calls for a disintegrating art, one that counters the "body dogmatic" and thereby the oversimplifying assertiveness of societal establishment.[6] The perfect corrective to the dogmatism (the absolute demands) of the physical body and the "body politic" would not be a specific heretical counterpart to the momentary orthodoxy; for a slight turn of fortune might easily institute the present heresy as the new orthodoxy: and because, moreover, a heretic idea in some sense becomes an established ideology if it is shared and firmly entertained even by a marginal minority group only. What is required is a radical anti-dogmatism, something like Keats's "Negative Capability," Mann's "sympathy with the abyss," de Gourmont's skepticism, irony, Rueckert's "both/and doctrine"—in short, syncretism, an embracing and maintaining of contraries. This attitude is close to the "sense of variousness and possibility" which characterizes the humanism and liberalism of Lionel Trilling.[7]

In this light it becomes clear that a radical spirit of opposition—not simple repudiation—and universal syncretism are just the two sides of the same coin; distinguishing them is mainly a matter of placing the emphases differently. Therefore, Burke is not inconsistent when, in his later work, he aims for an inclusive certainty, however skeptically grounded. In fact, the unattainability, for a limited human being, of a universal *coincidentia oppositorum*, man's inability to form, out of the divergent material of the world, an absolutely valid, coherent mental universe, necessitates a permanent quest for certainty, a "perpetual grailism," which is the motivation of Burke's intellectual work, just as it is the imaginative principle of *The White Oxen*.

Counter-Statement emphasizes the *oppositional* aspect of syncretism. Progressively focusing this antagonistic attitude upon specific political and sociological conditions, the book foreshadows Burke's temporary alignment with the left-wing radicalism of the 1930's. By analyzing the book *diachronically*, by following through its development, much of what might appear as a flat contradiction in any *synchronical* analysis will appear as the cumulative elaboration of a critical theory striving to encompass opposite viewpoints. There are explicit signs of this developmental aspect in the text itself. Thus, the later "Lexicon Rhetoricae," for example, is offered as a "codification, amplification, and correction" of two previous essays (CS, 123); and in this light the modal verb in the statement from the preface, according to which the book "should serve to elucidate a point of view," takes on a high degree of tentativeness with regard to the unity of the doctrine of *Counter-Statement.* Nevertheless, the permanent features behind the changing perspectives are equally important for a proper assessment of Burke's early critical theory.

V *The Composition of* Counter-Statement

Three phases may conveniently be distinguished in the essays collected in the book. (1) The earliest and most purely "esthetic" piece is "Three Adepts of 'Pure' Literature," based on individual essays on de Gourmont, Flaubert, and Pater, two of which had appeared in the *Dial* (1921, 1922) and one in *1924* (1924). The significant rearrangements and changes of emphasis made for the inclusion in the book clearly indicate the developmental aspect of Burke's criticism. (2) The second group of essays, which is the most important one from the point of view of a basic contribution to critical theory in general, includes "Psychology and Form" (*Dial,* 1925) and "The Poetic Process" (*Guardian,* 1925). Because of the close thematic coherence, they must be discussed together with "Lexicon Rhetoricae." "The Status of Art" is also relevant in this context. (3) Historically, however, "Lexicon" belongs to the last group together with "Thomas Mann and André Gide" (*Bookman,* 1930), "Program," and "Applications of the Terminology" (which, in a different arrangement, was serialized as "Redefinitions" in *The New Republic,* 1931). Thematically, "Program" (written after 1929) is the most unequivocal plea for a *littérature engagée,* a literature of political side-taking.

Although these three temporal phases of the making of *Counter-Statement* do not correspond one-to-one with the book's changing thematic concerns, the three main themes nevertheless become progressively articulate. The development is from a defense of poetry against various detractors in the social environment through a strictly ergocentric ("esthetic") theory of form to a program for an artistic attack upon the social scene. Thus seemingly coming round 180 degrees from the initial estheticism, Burke's critical thought nevertheless is consistent, as will presently become clear.

VI *What Is "Pure" Literature?*

With the essay on Mann and Gide and with some passages on Oswald Spengler in "Status," "Adepts" is important insofar as it documents the main early influences, both imaginative and critical, on Kenneth Burke. The essay reveals his primary interest in considerations of literary theory. His interpretation of Flaubert's, Pater's, and de Gourmont's opinions capitalizes on the Nietzschean traits in their esthetic theories, particularly the peculiarly ambivalent art/life alignment which, especially in de Gourmont's thought, is enlarged into a confrontation of intelligence with the life of the senses, with the body. Following Flaubert's lead, the French critic actually reversed the received idea according to which the standard of art is its societal usefulness. For as he sees it, intellectual pursuits alone distinguish man from other organisms, and therefore social institutions are deemed useful only insofar as they make intellectual (and hence artistic) pursuits possible (CS, 17). Burke fully endorses this view, and he thus enrolls himself in the *l'art pour l'art* school of the *fin de siècle* Decadents, on whose convictions he founded his own critical theory. But, as this creed implies that art is necessarily subversive, the essential antinomianism of Burke's criticism proves to be inherent in the very foundation of his esthetic.[8]

It may be noted in passing that the apparent terminological inconsistencies in these considerations are characteristic of the tradition in which Burke's criticism becomes crystallized. Literature, art, and intellectual pursuit in general become in a sense synonymous; and, although the rigor of such a position would have to reject Pater's inclusion of the tasting of wine and the inhaling of the fragrance of herbs among the esthetic pleasures, it would have to accept all "artistic and accomplished forms of human life" as manifestations of art.[9] This extension of the range of critical considerations beyond the realm of what some strict theorists regard as literature or art presupposes a pragmatic view of a continuity among all mental activities and foreshadows

Burke's later concern with devising a critical method amenable to an analysis of linguistic documents of all kinds.

Thus, in the formative phase of his esthetic theory, Burke adheres to a strict art-for-art's-sake position in the tradition of de Gourmont.[10] Literature for him is therefore autonomous (disinterested); and yet at the same time it is intimately bound up with life. It is autonomous insofar as it exploits to the fullest the resources of its medium, language—not in view of moral, political, scientific or other ulterior ends, but as an end in itself. Literature is bound up with life in a number of ways: by drawing upon it; adding to it; opposing it; and, in so doing, by being life's supreme occupation. Hence Burke's formula: literature is the "*verbalization* of experience." By contrast, Naturalism, he feels, rules out the autonomous aspect of literature and shifts the emphasis so completely to the "verbalization of *experience*" that it breaks up the dialectical tension between autonomy and lifelikeness and suppresses the former.

Thus Burke condemns what he feels to be Stendhal's "art-to-conceal-art"; and quite consistently, he praises Flaubert for practicing an "art-to-display-art." The latter is strictly anti-utilitarian. In this context, Burke of course quotes Flaubert's famous *dictum* that the ideal book for him is one which has almost no content and is sustained by nothing but style. It is significant that, in the original version of the Flaubert essay, Burke emphatically uses this statement as the climax of his argument; but, in the *Counter-Statement* version, it is incorporated elsewhere in the text, and the Flaubert section concludes with the observation that Flaubert's terms for making this distinction—"pure form" versus "pure matter"—blur the issue. Burke rephrases the problem in terms of declamation, ritual, and ceremony as against realism, observation, and information, thus heralding his own later theories.

Art-to-display-art requires a thoroughly rhetorical, an ostentatiously "written" style, one that emphasizes the medium. This is why Burke is in full sympathy with Flaubert's *éperduments de style* (raptures of style) experienced when he wrote *La Tentation de Saint-Antoine*, the only book which, according to Flaubert's *Correspondence*, fully satisfied its author. For this reason, Burke is also attracted by Pater's work and his esthetic thought; and this is why one can discover distinct echoes of de Gourmont in "Three

Adepts," of de Gourmont, who bluntly and yet wilily proclaimed: "There are two types of writers, those who write and those who don't." [11] Rhetoric in all its aspects has become a dominant and lasting concern of Burke's criticism.

But this is also true of the corresponding aspect, that of the ties of art with life. With Burke, this concern almost amounts to a biologism of art. Dwelling long upon the sensualistic anthropology of de Gourmont, who recognizes the intellect as the specifically human attribute but regards it as rooted in the life of the senses and, ultimately, in physiology, Burke endorses the view that art, intellectual activity, is fully justified simply because it satisfies an appetite of man, the intelligent animal. A key essay for clarifying this issue is de Gourmont's "La Dissociation des Idées." [12] Briefly, in this essay the progress of culture is equated with the free play of the intellect in analyzing and dissecting "received ideas," conventional verities, which common desires and interests have previously associated. This concept of dissociation has had an enormous influence on Burke, and his basic approach to art and life, his method of "perspective by incongruity," directly depends on de Gourmont's slightly different maneuvers.

Another earlier and more direct sign of this influence is the essay, "Thomas Mann and André Gide," itself a delightful exercise in dissociation (CS, 92–106). Aptly differentiating the two writers' common theme both from Mann's ethical conscientiousness and Gide's esthetic villainy, Burke is able to show that the "underlying situation" of the two authors' works is the same fascination with "the repellent, the diseased, the degenerate"; the differences are a matter of presentational strategy. Ultimately, Mann's "irony" and Gide's "curiosity" are identical as attempts at humanizing the state of doubt. Moreover, in a passage newly written for the *Counter-Statement* version of this essay, Burke regrets that de Gourmont has not carried his analysis of "clusters of associations" into literary criticism; in *The Philosophy of Literary Form* Burke later does exactly that.

Yet it must equally be borne in mind that de Gourmont's emphasis on the intellect is not so rigorously rationalistic, not so intellectually abstract as the term itself might be taken to imply. The pressure of the tradition of Nietzschean and Bergsonian anti-Idealism asserts itself; there are even elements of a dormant pragmatism in such views as de Gourmont's conception of a truth as a commonly held belief. Also, his concept of "intellect" has strong psychological overtones, and it could easily be shown how his dissociations are tinged by his own "desires and interests"—how, simultaneously with his overt dissociations, he sneaks in covert associations of his own.

De Gourmont's "intellectualism," therefore, is in a way anti-intellectualistic; or, rather, his—and Burke's—thought is characterized by an "intellectual" kind of anti intellectualism. There is thus a sense in which the intellect in Burke's theory of art is connected with life, with biology, by a secret underground shortcut, so to speak. Traces at least of an uncritical reconciliation can be discerned. One aspect of this shortcut is that Burke discusses only the psychosomatically emotive aspect of art, banning all intellectual, cognitive elements; this statement is in no way to imply, however, that his discussion is not highly intellectual and intellectually stimulating.

Primarily, however, the two realms—of *logos* and *bios*, mind and body, art and life—for him are characterized by the relationship of sustained tension alluded to above. As in the thought and work of Thomas Mann, "pure" art for Burke is the result of an almost desperate intellectual endeavor of accepting life by staking out a realm against life. Imaginatively, Mann's Tonio Kröger and Burke's Prince Llan are not-so-distant cousins; critically, the definition of form as audience *appetite* is a logical corollary of this view.

VII *A Psychological Formalism*

These considerations concerning the relationship of art and life lead to the second major theme of *Counter-Statement:* the theory of form. Unless one embraces the statistical methods of information theory wholeheartedly and reduces a formal analysis to the measuring and comparing of strictly quantitative features of a given text, there is no way of banning psychological considerations from criticism. A literary work is essentially connected with its author and its audience. Aspects of both these ratios are the elements of Burke's perspectivistic theory of form as developed in "Psychology and Form" and in "The Poetic Process," which are equally brilliant as esthetic speculation and as essays. Since "Lexicon Rhetoricae," which is frankly intended as a "judgment machine," [13] codifies and modifies the views developed in the two earlier essays, Burke's psychological formalism is best presented systematically by minimizing the developmental factor except where later corrections are representative of the trend of Burke's thought.

(a) *Causes of literary appeal.* As has been shown, Burke's analysis of the scene from *Hamlet* pivots around such audience-oriented categories as suspense, withholding of information, juxtaposition, contrast, surprise, and fulfilment of a promise. In fact, his total theory of form hinges upon the central question: What makes literary works emotionally appealing? (CS, esp. ix, 123). He finds two sources of appeal: the symbol embedded in the literary structure, and the sequence or arrangement of such a symbol and its ramifications. Now there is nothing striking in the observation that both the content and the form of a literary work can be interesting, attractive. The importance of Burke's theory resides in the exact mode of redefining these two conventional principles, which makes it possible to overcome the "seeming breach between form and subject-matter, between technique and psychology" (CS, 31); in the precise distinction of types of literary appeal; and in his personal preferences for one definite type. Ultimately, his concept of form as audience psychology transcends conventional types of formalism.[14]

(b) *Symbol: emotional and technical form.* The primary redefinition, on the "content" side of Burke's esthetic theory, is his introduction of the term "symbol" (or rather, "ramifications of the symbol") as an equivalent for subject matter (CS, 49, 50, 158, *passim*). This association was prepared for by his early interest in the Symbolists and by his conviction that "psychoanalysis is the scientific counterpart of symbolist art" (CS, 21). The theory justifying this view is Burke's underlying psychological perspectivism. For from the point of view of author psychology, the symbol is the verbalization of a pattern of experience (CS, 152), of an oppressive syndrome, as it were; it is "spontaneously generated," like a dream; and as such it serves as the germ of a plot, or as the idea for a poem (CS, 56).

But unlike a dream, the resultant work is also decisively determined by considerations of audience psychology and technical requirements: the poet attains "articulacy by linking his emotion to a technical form" (*ibid.*). Self-expression, communication, and—implicitly—a kind of objective perfectibility, though originating in a common core, are the divergent powers that cooperate to create a work of art. To illustrate: there is a poet who has the feeling that he is undeservedly neglected. He may then "externalize his suffering" in the symbol of "The King and the Peasant" which he will develop in such a way as to show, in the end, that the king is a boor, and the peasant the real king. But his very strategy will make it necessary to introduce material that in itself is diametrically opposed to this over-all purpose: in order to make the fall of the king impressive and *convincing to the audience*, he will have to introduce court scenes that first show the king in all his royal splendor (CS, 57–58).

Such *technical* considerations, which also include the fact that the given symbol virtually requires the work to be a fairy tale, are at odds with the *emotional* form of the symbol, to which they contribute only in a roundabout way—by interrupting the emotional consistency to add "salience" (CS, 51), *technical* form, "decoration." These features distinguish the work of art from a dream, from a mere "uttering of emotion" on the part of the author, and make it an "evocation of [the audience's] emotion." To use a different metaphor: "If, as humans, we cry out that we are Napoleon, as artists we seek to command an army" (CS, 53). Springing from the same germ, emotion (expression) and technique (treatment) coexist in a work of art insofar as the poet "translates his emotions into a mechanism for arousing emotion in others" (CS, 55). Mark Twain thus "transformed the bitterness that he *wanted* to utter into the humor that he *could* evoke" (CS, 53)—a fact which accounts for the acrimony of much of his humor. Therefore, "in that fluctuating region between pure emotion and pure decoration, humanity and craftsmanship, utterance and performance, lies the field of art, the evocation of emotion by mechanism, a norm which, like all norms, is a conflict become fusion" (CS, 56).

In this formula, the term "fusion" emphasizes the unity of the finished product to such an extent as to belittle its compositeness more than is warranted. Otherwise, this concise definition of art is dialectically well shaped. Insofar as it embraces the human element, it is superior to Eliot's early "catalyst" theory of composition. John Crowe Ransom has later submitted an almost *verbatim* reformulation of this definition, while avoiding the simplification of "fusion." [15]

(c) *The limited appeal of emotional form.* Art, then, is characterized by this emotion/technique dialectic. Thus, if one imagines someone expressing his feeling of undeserved neglect by continuously muttering, "The king is a boor, and I am the real king," his outcry would only have the perfect consistency of *emotional* form. This ramification of the symbol would be hopelessly itself, but would not be art; it might be a sign of mental derangement (CS, 158). Even so, it would contain a *modicum* of technical form, however unintentional: a series. Pure emotional form is a nonexistent abstraction. On the other hand, a literary work of art that bristles with technique does not therefore relinquish emotional form. To the extent that the initial symbol is elaborated in a work, extended, and repeated, the work as a whole is "symbolic," or characteristic, or representative of both its author (CS, 58) and of its era (CS, 87): it "applies to life" insofar as the symbol verbalizes experience (CS, 61). And insofar as the reader shares the underlying experience, the mere ramification of the symbol, the "emotional form" alone, may appeal to him.

To be precise: "technical form" has its emotional aspect, too. After all, emotional *effect* is the dominant category of Burke's esthetic. However, the epithet of "emotional form" refers to the author's original emotion as immediately expressed through the symbol and its consistent ramifications: to the "Byronism," for instance, of Byron. This purely symbolic or emotional appeal would be attractive (that is to say, beautiful) only for persons who are emotionally predisposed to a syndrome similar to that of the author—for "mute [potential] Byrons" (CS, 58). In extreme cases, it may be added, a work of mainly symbolic appeal could be permanently attractive for *aficionados,* for fans, if it does not have any other distinction; but its attraction for neutral readers could only be a matter of curiosity. Once it has imparted its message, it would lose all its interest for them.

(d) *Fact, information, science.* Burke does not take the special case of the *aficionado* into account, but he assumes that in all cases the symbol loses its intrinsic attractiveness when its news value is spent. For, assuming as he does that it verbalizes a pattern of experience, he identifies it with the "diagnosis," or simplification, of a situation which "attracts us [emotionally] by its power of formula, exactly as a theory of history or science" (CS, 58). In this way, Burke comes to associate symbol, subject matter, fact, information, and science with the "intrinsic" interest (CS, 33) of a given detail of a work. Nevertheless, a theory of science may remain intellectually absorbing; but once having been read and understood, it must lose, Burke seems to assume, the quality of direct emotional appeal which he so prizes in art. The ascendancy of science, Burke feels, has brought about exactly such an almost exclusive interest in information; and, consequently, this development has led even the artist to stress "fact" in Naturalistic works. These considerations reveal one of the main motives for Burke's defense of art against the inroads of science.

Yet his attitude toward science is more complex than simple repudiation. To be sure, he rejects it whenever it detracts from art; but he argues that there need not be a fundamental opposition between art and science (CS, 199). He even identifies scientific method with skepticism (CS, 202)—his very principle of Humanism, or Stoicism (cf. above, Chapter 3, IV). In a sense, Burke attempts to defend art by adapting scientific methods to it without sacrificing art's independent, esthetic nature. Following the basic distinctions but not the overt intentions of C. K. Ogden and I. A. Richards in *The Meaning of Meaning* (1923), Burke later works toward a "science of symbolism" in *Permanence and Change* (1935), and in *The Philosophy of Literary Form* (1941) he adapts psychoanalytical methods to this end.

From the point of view of his development, the psychologism of *Counter-Statement* is an adequate preparation. This early volume of criticism also resembles Richards' *Principles of Literary Criticism* (1924), a book written with virtually the same underlying "pattern of experience" and employing an almost identical stratagem—a defense of poetry against science by employing scientific, quantitative criteria, notably in Richards' psychological theory of value and complexity. This coincidence reinforces the diagnosis of a common climate of ideas; for Richards and Burke worked independently of each other. When the *Principles* appeared, the core of Burke's theory of form had already been written; it was published shortly afterwards.[16] Psychology-oriented and pragmatically-minded as both critics are, it is not strange that they should have developed similar tactics and even similar formulas for locating the center of their respective esthetic theories in the audience.

(e) *Technical form: the necessary counter-principle.* If the scientific emphasis on the detail as *intrinsically* interesting commands only a transitory appeal—that of newness, of *discovery*—it follows that art, to be permanent, must marshal other means of attraction. Burke takes his cue from the "art of the great ages (Aeschylus, Shakespeare, Racine)" which, he feels, keeps the intrinsic interest reduced to its properly minor position and relies for its effects primarily upon the *extrinsic,* contextual use of details, upon their function in a pattern of disclosure, of natural *recovery:* that is, upon ritual (CS, 33). Such a ritual, or performance, necessarily involves the conscious or repressed awareness on the part of the performer of the audience. Therefore, in this phase of Burke's critical theory, the communicative aspect—the consideration of the audience's psychology—becomes more important than the expressive aspect, or author psychology.

The shift that Burke's terminology undergoes at this point is telling enough: in "Lexicon," the new term "emotional connective" replaces "emotional form" (CS, 159). This change makes it possible to use *form* without qualification (instead of "technical form") as a term for the audience-oriented aspect of a literary work, although remnants of "emotional form" continue to persist, as presently becomes clear. *Form,* then, is the "creation of an appetite in the mind of the auditor, and the adequate satisfying of that appetite" (CS, 31); this satisfaction may be heightened by a "temporary set of frustrations." "A work has form in so far as one part of it leads a reader to anticipate another part, and to be gratified by the sequence" (CS, 124).

(f) *Aspects of form.* Though necessarily interrelated and allowing of combinations, five aspects of form may be distinguished: two of them Burke calls "progressive"; the other three are: "repetitive," "conventional," and "minor." [17]

(i) *Syllogistic progression,* according to Burke, is involved in all closely knit plot constructions or arguments. Poe's stories of ratiocination and the tragic analyses of Ibsen's Naturalistic dramas employ this form in its purity. (It is from this syllogistic progression that Burke's later principle of "objective perfectibility" or "consummation" are derived.) In a well-made plot, this sequence is, of course, not utterly deterministic since it usually includes a reversal scene in which the audience's expectations are changed completely. Thus, Brutus' speech in *Julius Caesar* (III.ii) serves to prepare for his exoneration, but Antony's speech over Caesar's body immediately afterwards heralds his downfall (CS, 124).

Burke does not continue to explore this relationship between probable expectations and necessary results; to do so would probably require a modification of the term "syllogistic"; for in sheer procedure the closely knit plot and the logical proof, despite their similarities, differ decisively. A syllogism, or, for instance, a Euclidian proof, is *totally* determined, and properly so; but a play, to the extent that its construction should be thus forseeable even in its minor movements, loses its esthetic value: if a play's prospective and retrospective aspects coincide in each moment, it is reduced to a formula of no formal appeal. It is therefore important to differentiate between the logical process of syllogistic progression and the imaginative progression of the closely knit plot type. Burke's failure to make this distinction at this point foreshadows his explicit fusion of logical procedure and imaginative association in *Permanence and Change* (cf. below, Chapter 5, Section V); it enables him to identify ideologies as "collective poems" in *Attitudes toward History,* and it leads him to slight the difference between dialectic and drama (cf. below, Chapter 8, Section III a).

(ii) *Qualitative progression* lacks the pronounced anticipatory nature of "syllogistic" progression and satisfies the reader when he recognizes "rightness after the event" (CS, 125). The transition from the grotesque seriousness of the murder scene in *Macbeth* to the grotesque buffoonery of the porter scene is a supreme instance of qualitative progression.

(iii) "*Repetitive form* is the consistent maintaining of a principle under new guises" (CS, 125). Burke fails to explicate that this principle is closely related to the *subject matter* aspect of "ramification" by which the initial symbol is amplified or restated by new but consistent details. To be sure, rhyme and rhythm, which cannot be classified as subject matter, are also manifestations of repetitive form; they are devices of power which, overdone, may result in monotony. Burke diagnoses the same power/monotony dialectic strictly in connection with the ramification of the symbol (CS, 160). Repetitive form therefore functions as a very inclusive principle. It may be added that at the same time it is intimately interconnected with qualitative progression. For, by emphasizing the new guises, one can transpose repetition into progression; and, by emphasizing the common theme, one can turn qualitative progression into repetition, as when one would stress the grotesqueness common to both the murder scene and the porter scene in *Macbeth.* In a different context, Burke himself analyzes rhyme as such a hybrid form which repeats certain speech sounds while it substitutes others ("room"—"doom," CS, 142). This easy convertability reinforces the diagnosis of Burke's models of form not as types but as *aspects.*

(iv) "*Conventional form* involves to some degree the appeal of form *as form*" (CS, 126), the "categorical expectancy" anterior to the actual process of reading (CS, 127). One has, for instance, certain very clear-cut expectations when turning to a sonnet or a Beethoven symphony. And it should be added to Burke's considerations that categorical expectancy more than any other form depends upon audience "psychology"—depends, to be precise, on audience experience and intelligence. For it is evident that a sophisticated reader who knows both tradition and convention will categorically expect many things *anterior to* the actual experience; a less trained reader, however, may form his anticipations only *during the process* of reading. Thus for many, the theophany at the end of a Euripidean tragedy will be just as much a matter of anterior anticipation as the multiple weddings that terminate a typical Shakespearean comedy, but others might—if at all—recognize the rightness of these endings only after the event: in extreme cases, one man's conventional form will be another man's qualitative progression.[18] Relativism is the necessary corollary of any esthetic of effect; Richards' postulate of the "right kind of reader" is no solution of this dilemma[19]—but neither is a dismissal of audience considerations from esthetics on the grounds that they raise more problems than they can possibly solve, that a psychologistic esthetic must necessarily result in anarchy.[20] The ultimate consequence of postulating a separate ontological status of the literary work is a complete "dehumanization of art" that invites purely statistical, quantitative criteria of analysis.

(v) *Minor or incidental forms,* finally, occur when the other types of form are carried down from the gross structure into the line-by-line texture so that dramatic speeches become plays in themselves, images form a progressive series, and so on. Such minor forms—"metaphor, paradox, disclosure, reversal, contraction, expansion, bathos, apostrophe, series, chiasmus" (CS, 127)—play an important part in defining *eloquence,* the "god-term" (GM, 43, 53, *passim*) or ultimate principle of Burke's formalism; therefore, they take on a particular importance (cf. below, Section VII,i).

(g) *Interrelation and conflict of forms.* As has been shown, these five aspects of form necessarily interpenetrate and overlap. They are no rigid categorics of classification (types), but tools of description which may serve to bring out the complexity of a scene. Thus, Burke speaks of the "vigorous presence of all five aspects" in the catastrophe of *Othello* (V.ii.341–59): victimage at the end of a tragedy involves categorical expectancy; the suicide is the necessary outcome of Othello's predicaments (syllogistic progression); at the same time, the rashness of the act is in keeping with Othello's tempestuous character (repetitive form); the sacrificial mood adds to the feeling of gloomy forebodings implied in the previous scenes (qualitative progression, again merging upon repetition); and the speech has the form of a tiny plot (minor form).

Forms may also conflict in many ways. One striking example is that of a character's radical reform for the sake of the syllogistic progression of the over-all argument, thus violating repetitive form. The author will usually try to justify such a reversal as a higher insight drawn from the character's previous experience. He may succeed in doing so: the dcvclopmcnt of Jurgis Rudkus (in Upton Sinclair's *The Jungle,* 1906) from a family-regarding worker in the Chicago meat-packing industry to a class-conscious proletarian is certainly convincing within the frame of the novel. Nevertheless, formally one can register the conflict between progression and repetition—a necessary conflict, not a cause for censure.

(h) *Priority and individuation of forms.* Insofar as repetitive form contains, among other things, symbolic "charges," the five aspects of form, as Burke conceives of them, cover the whole range of literary appeal as the "*conditions of emotional response*" (CS, 47).[21] Of course, forms do not appeal simply as definitions, as they are presented here, but only when a certain subject matter is arranged accordingly. As universal (intellectual) principles, they can only be understood; in order to be experienced, they must be embodied in particular material. Burke here appropriates a scholastic principle to esthetics, "*universale intellegitur, singulare sentitur*" (CS, 47)—universals are understood, particulars are felt.

But, according to Burke, these forms are not only conceptual tools for literary analysis. They have an existential priority: "They apply to art, since they apply outside of art" (CS, 141). Various natural phenomena, such as the ripening of crops, or the phases of an epidemic, are experienced as progressions—have the nature of progression—are the "material of progressive form." Burke wavers between these formulations (CS, 45, 141), but he at any rate postulates a pre-existence of such forms in the mind. As "innate forms of the mind," they are the "potentials for being interested in certain processes or arrangements" such as "crescendo, contrast, comparison, balance, repetition, disclosure, reversal, contraction, expansion, magnification, series, and so on" (CS, 46).

The five aspects of form previously discussed subsume these innate forms. Crescendo is clearly a type of progression, probably syllogistic because it involves an element of anticipation; contrast can probably best be regarded as qualitative progression, whereas repetition cannot help but be repetitive form. Because of the interpenetration of the aspects of form, such a classification can never be systematic, only pragmatic—which is not necessarily a disadvantage.

The postulate of pre-existent forms of the mind "inherent in the very germ-plasma of man" is a hypothesis in the etymological sense of the word. The basis of Burke's esthetic is a biological—precisely, a psychosomatic—Platonism, a more biologically oriented variant of the Metapsychology which Freud envisaged in *The Psychopathology of Everyday Life* (1904, English transl. 1938).[22] On this primordial level, art and life are non-distinctively interconnected: simply by charting the natural progression of a sunrise or the progressive stages in a cholera epidemic (as in Mann's *Death in Venice*), the artist exercises "form" (CS, 45). This art/life continuity is completely in line with one aspect of Burke's estheticism, that of art as "bound up with life." The other aspect, art's difference, must now be explored with regard to its implications for formalism.

(i) *Eloquence as the essence of art.* It has been established that all informative works—those relying primarily on subject matter interest—tend to lose their potentiality for arresting the reader's emotions after the first reading, except, perhaps, in the case of an *aficionado.* But even the formal, technical appeal of certain works can fade if the interest centers predominantly on plot suspense and surprise. Burke surprisingly singles out Stendhal as the example of a merely "informative," non-eloquent writer; Upton Sinclair and E. M. Remarque, for instance, would perhaps come closer to this type.

The best way, therefore, of assuring artistic permanence, Burke feels, is to carry the mechanisms of appeal from the over-all block-by-block structure of a work into its line-by-line texture. Thus, after successively rejecting subject matter and gross structure (plot), he locates formal excellence and hence permanence in minor form, in style, in *eloquence.* "Thus, those elements of surprise and suspense are subtilized, carried down into the writing of a line or a sentence, until in all its smallest details the work bristles with disclosures, contrasts, restatements with a difference, ellipses, images, aphorism, volume, sound-values, in short all the complex wealth of minutiae which in their line-for-line aspect we call style and in their broader outlines we call form" (CS, 37–38). An excellent example of such eloquence adduced by Burke is the shift of tone at the end of Section II of T. S. Eliot's *The Waste Land,* where the transition from the sultry type of "Goonight. Ta ta. Goonight" to a poetic "Good night, ladies, good night, sweet ladies, good night, good night" has, apart from the Shakespearean echo, almost the quality of the harmonic resolution of a discord (CS, 39).

On the other hand, Burke misreads the end of Karel Čapek's *R.U.R.,* where the Robot, prompted by the "dawn of love," stammers his first lyrical observations. Burke's complaint that "one could do nothing but wring his hands at the absence of the aesthetic mould which produced the overslung 'speeches' of Romeo and Juliet" (CS, 38) bespeaks a surprising error of judgment based on an undue slighting of thematic coherence, the consistency of the subject. After all, the Robot had only quite recently turned human; and it would have been against all probability and propriety to have him speak, as it were, with a long rhetorical and sentimental tradition in his bolts. Should he perhaps speak in the high-sounding accents in which Mary Shelley made Frankenstein's monster discourse with Victor on the glacier of Montanvert after less than a year of an autodidactic *education sentimentale?*

(j) *The universality of eloquence.* Such an erroneous estimation of the ending of Čapek's *R.U.R.* reveals both the historical situation in which the esthetic of *Counter-Statement* was formulated and Burke's personal taste. For, while it is no doubt true that eloquence is the essence of art—or that "art, at least in the great periods when it has flowered, was the conversion, or transcendence, of emotion into eloquence, and was thus a factor added to life" (CS, 41)—it is no less true that the euphuistic style that Burke admired, justified, and practiced, notably in his novel, *Towards a Better Life*, is only *one* of the many possibilities of eloquence.

Hemingway's Naturalistic prose, for example, frequently has an eloquence, a rhetoric of its own, although a quite different one. Especially his late novel *The Old Man and the Sea* bears a completely Burkean analysis: there is the initial symbol and its consistent ramification—Santiago's streak of bad luck as a fisherman; there is the "technical form"—the arrangement that involves recalcitrant material and serves to render the incidents powerful—in his changing fortune in handling the marlin. Both these elements cooperate to create a crescendo; in fact, they are so intimately connected as to project an ambiguous attitude: victory through defeat. To be sure, the work achieves eloquence not by any "overslung speeches" but by a precise and pleasing understatement—by silence, the "'flowering' of information" (CS, 38).

To the extent that Burke's method is applicable to works which he would probably exclude, his defense of eloquence is irrefutable; but his hanging an Albatross about the neck of Naturalism is a historical coincidence and a matter of taste. Therefore, when these personal preferences are established as principles, the result is not always persuasive; and striking and important insights are sometimes vitiated by such restrictions. By a logical and most convincing extension of the definition of form as audience psychology, Burke aptly defines art as the waking dream of the audience, "while the artist oversees the conditions which determine the dream. He is the manipulator of blood, brains, heart and bowels which, while we sleep, dictate the mould of our desires" (CS, 36–37).

In this context, Burke has skillfully and critically adapted the Freudian concept of art as the pipedream of the neurotic. But the artist is not artistic *qua* neurotic, as Edmund Wilson seems almost to argue in *The Wound and the Bow* (1941); in Burke, there is just as much the recognition that a man may become a neurotic *qua* artist—an un-Freudian insight which C. G. Jung later formulates in "Psychology and Literature." [23] Yet when, as in "Psychology and Form," Burke relies *exclusively* on the audience-psychological aspect, he comes even verbally very close to describing successful art as somniferous: "Music, then, fitted less than any other art for imparting information, deals minutely in frustrations and fulfillments of desire, and for that reason more often gives us those curves of emotion which, because they are natural, can bear repetition without loss. It is for this reason that music, like folk tales, is most capable of lulling us to sleep" (CS, 36). In this statement Burke allows his theory of form to slip back below the dialectical precision it has already approached in such definitions as that of art as a dualism of emotion and decoration, utterance and performance. But such a reductionism is the inherent danger of an esthetic based on the single criterion of emotional effect, which slights the role that the antithetical intellectual material of theme, thought, character, and significance plays in an art that does *not* put the audience to sleep.

(k) *Esthetic truth.* The exact nature of the price Burke has to pay for his insights into the psychological aspects of literary form can perhaps be best specified by examining his differing definitions of esthetic truth. Early, in "Psychology and Form," the confrontation of the scientific as discovery and the artistic as recovery led to the following assertion: "Truth in art is not the discovery of facts, not an addition to human knowledge in the scientific sense of the word. It is, rather, the exercise of human propriety, the formulation of symbols which rigidify our sense of poise and rhythm. Artistic truth is the externalization of taste" (CS, 42).

The instances of propriety in art which Burke gives are invariably examples of consistency of details; the point of view is strictly upon relationships *within* the work. Ulysses' adventure in the cave of Polyphemus does not impart any factual information *about* one-eyed ogres, but allows only for the following statement: "Given the companions of Ulysses in the cave of Polyphemus, it is true that they would escape clinging to the bellies of the herd led out to pasture" (CS, 43). This "truth" of an immanent propriety—even though scientifically inaccurate—Burke calls the "emotional rightness" of art. But such a criterion is hardly more than one of subjective satisfaction: indeed, Burke sets it off against the "entirely intellectual" nature of the pragmatic test in science (CS, 42n)—an opposition which is too simplistic in its rigor.

No doubt this distinction between two different aspects of truth as revealed in science and in art is fundamentally correct; but it would require intricate elaborations. For the "science" aspect, one would have to begin by considering that, while it is true that an (intellectual) hypothesis always *controls* the setup of an empirical experiment, it does at the same time *subject* itself to the authority of the experimental test. On the "art" side, the starting point would probably be to note that, while the instigator of the experiment is emotion, both the intellect (theme, thought) and realistic detail (character, "nature") serve as authorities of correction; but the over-all appearance of the finished product may be said to possess something of the "naturalness" of a natural object—a quality which critics usually refer to in terms of the "muteness," "dumbness" of a work of art: it "does not mean," it "is"; but, just by *being*, it has, of course, a meaning—a "truth." [24] Yet to define this artistic truth in terms of emotion, propriety, taste, and poise is meaningful only in the specific situation of anti-scientific defense; if the situation changes, the idea, if still adhered to, will freeze into ideology. As Burke later stated in connection with a moderate defense of Rousseauism: "Any principles can lead to vast absurdities, if only because principles persist and grow in popularity long after they have gained the end for which they were formulated" (CS, 186). This admission is not to imply that Burke's definition of esthetic truth was absurd at the outset; it is to assert that changes become necessary—and some such modifications are made in "Lexicon." The over-all principle continues to be immanent propriety ("consistency"); the factor of referential, scientific meaning is introduced in a very roundabout way by equating "fact" with "belief" based on magical, religious, or scientific "revelation": "Art enters when this revelation is ritualized, when it is converted into a symbolic process" (CS, 168).

This ritualizing of revelation brings about a "kind of metaphorical truth." Scientific truth, Burke seems to presuppose, applies to the straightforward formulation of a "pattern of experience"—experience as it arises out of the relationship between an organism and its environment (cf. CS, 150–51, 42; PC, 5–6)—but metaphorical truth consists of making a fact (belief) convincing to the audience. Even if the poet does not share this belief, "saliency" may require him to present it convincingly: "A poet may base an effect upon a belief which he knows to be false; just as he may compose a poem on riding to the moon; in either case he writes 'as if' the underlying fact were true" (CS, 169). Consistency, effectiveness, the power to convince—it is difficult for an esthetic of effect to go beyond such categories of *belief,* just as it is difficult for an esthetic of essence to avoid the pitfall of a rigoristic *doctrinairism,* as when, in the Hegelian formula, "Das Schöne bestimmt sich . . . als der sinnliche Schein der Idee," some critics stress idea, truth, to the exclusion of the element of "*Schein.*" [25] In connection with his discussion of the social function of art in *Counter-Statement,* Burke returns to this problem of esthetic truth in order to bring out yet different aspects.

(1) *The changing meaning of "Symbol."* This rephrasing of, and adding to, the definition of esthetic truth is symptomatic of Burke's changing political outlook. Such considerations are still a part of esthetic formalism, as Burke develops the doctrine; but they demarcate the border of political science and sociology. Before stepping over this border and discussing the third main theme of *Counter-Statement*—the view of the socio-political function of art which Burke held at the time of writing the final essays of the book—it is important to give a very brief account of a significant change in the application of the term "symbol" in "Lexicon," for this modification prognosticates his later political preoccupations.

The symbol, it will be recalled, was introduced as the term for the spontaneously generated cluster of facts which express the nature of the poet's burden. As such, it faces two ways: toward the environment, which it (subjectively) diagnoses, and toward the poetic work, whose germ it is. As poetic idea, it embraces the possibilities of both expressive ramification (in keeping with author psychology) and technical formation (in view of audience psychology). It is this second element, *form,* which Burke stresses in the earlier phases of *Counter-Statement.*

Later, however, the term *symbol,* especially in its former meaning, gains more and more emphasis. A minute but significant case in point is that the word was never capitalized in the original "The Poetic Process" but is in the latter part of "Lexicon." A more conspicuous change is the suppression, in "Lexicon," of "spontaneous generation" as the manner of producing a symbol—another device for dignifying the term. In "Lexicon," the generation of the Symbol is described without modification as the "conversion of a pattern of experience into a Symbolic equivalent," a "formula for affecting an audience" (CS, 157). To the extent that in this definition the dialectical dualism between (symbolic) expression and (technical) evocation is dissolved in favor of the former, to the extent that the term "Symbolic equivalent of a pattern of experience" becomes a near-equivalent for the "finished work of art," the latent fusionism in Burke's thought again asserts itself.

In this context it is also important to note that Burke, in the later parts of *Counter-Statement,* places more emphasis on the *situation* itself as the generating principle of the Symbol. In "Status," for instance, he had insisted that art "reflects" a situation only in the sense that it "*adds* a solution" to it—it certainly is not caused by it (CS, 80, x); but in "Program" he notes that "the particularities of the cluster [of conditions] will *require* the stressing of some and the slighting of others [italics mine]." The shift is microscopic but decisive; with the previously mentioned revaluation of the symbolic aspect of a work, it helps to prepare for Burke's later analysis of literary works exclusively in terms of symbolic action, in terms of how a work is representative of its author's engrossments.

Another later device for the upgrading of a work's symbolic aspect is the redefinition of *eloquence.* In "Psychology and Form," eloquence stood for the subtilization of presentational devices (techniques), the carrying down of strategies of arrangement into the line-by-line texture, and thus was aligned with the formal aspect of a work (CS, 37–38). In "Lexicon," however, it is redefined as the frequency and vigor of both *symbolic and formal* effects, or "charges" (CS, 165, 181). In this definition, formal charges are effects of arrangement (CS, 164); but "symbolic intensity arises when the artist uses subject-matter 'charged' by the reader's situation outside the work of art" (CS, 163).

Although these revaluations of the Symbol as the aspect of a work which relates to extraneous situations are considerations of poetics proper, they distinctly point toward Burke's later political concerns with the social function of art. With the subsequent analysis of the essay "Program," the present discussion shifts over to the third main topic of *Counter-Statement,* "art and society."

VIII *The Political Activation of the Esthetic*

The purpose of "Program" is to "speculate as to which emotions and attitudes should be stressed, and which slighted, in the aesthetic adjustment to the particular conditions of today" (CS, 107) —of the Depression era. These speculations, Burke feels, do not touch the "absolute, unchanging purposes of the aesthetic"; but they do define their function in a given historical situation (CS, 107, 121). But the problem is whether such a political activation of the esthetic does not, in fact, modify its very nature.

(a) *The alignment of forces.* As for the historical situation, Burke's diagnosis can be paraphrased in the following, necessarily simplified way: the rise of applied science to organized mechanization and capitalist industrialism has "made the practical a menace" (CS, 110). A society based on an economy of mass production requires an efficient centralized government—an "ideal Fascism" (CS, 114) to which Burke is opposed. Such a political system must necessarily have ultimate faith in human virtue; for, based on an optimism in the perfectibility of efficiency, it is built on the assumption that the capable must rise to positions of centralized control, and that this control will be benevolent.

The esthete, equipped as he is with a special sensibility for experiencing the effects upon humanity of these mechanistic innovations, must furnish the "humanistic or cultural counterpart of the external changes brought about by industrialism, or mechanization" (CS, 108). His attitude is characterized by "acceptance"—an awareness of the innovations—but this "acceptance" does not necessarily mean "acquiescence" to them (CS, 108). He thus dissociates himself from the backwardness, the conservatism of the agrarian; but he at the same time recognizes that industrialism, despite its optimism in technical progress, is based on a superannuated principle—the pioneer glorification of toil, which the circumstances of overproduction and the concomitant enforced idleness have definitely turned into a harmful ideology (CS, 109).

These observations cause the esthete to cultivate negativism, the distrust of certainty, and hence of experimentalism, curiosity (CS, 111). Recognizing as he does that the optimism in universal virtue is unfounded, he comes to the conclusion that a "society is sound only if it can prosper on its vices, since virtues are by very definition rare and exceptional" (CS, 114). The ideal political organization, then, is diametrically opposed to "ideal Fascism"; it is an anarchic kind of democracy, a "colossal getting in one's own way," the "doctrine of interference" (CS, 115), of checks and balances. It is a kind of "Noah attitude": be prepared for the worst (CS, 113). This esthetico-Bohemian attitude is explicitly anti-mechanistic, anti-practical, anti-industrial, and as such "defensible because it could never triumph" (CS, 113).

Nevertheless, Burke propagates at least a partial practical triumph of his estheticism turned militant by supporting the Socialist-Marxist demand for a "generous spending of the industrialists' fortunes" by institutionalizing a "dole," a kind of negative tax to guarantee the minimal living expenses of everyone (CS, 115). But apparently Burke fails to see that this program perpetrates the very trust in the pioneer glorification of toil which he had censured as part of the backward orientation of the industrialist, for the dole can only function as long as there continues to be a majority of the pioneer-spirited people who devote themselves to toil as an end in itself. Thus, in the last analysis, it is impossible to base society on vice, indolence, inefficiency.

(b) *The limitations of a unilateral counter-statement.* But the practicability of the politico-economical program recommended by Burke, of which the dole is only one postulate, is not at issue here: the present concern is only with the consequences which the political engagement has for the *l'art pour l'art* position of Burke's esthetic. His theories are, as has been shown, originally characterized by the dialectical attitude of accepting life without acquiescing to it, by staking out an intellectual realm against the biological-neurological necessities without abandoning them. The basic attitude is a universal skepticism. The special recommendations of "Program" abandon the omnilateral nature of Burke's early estheticism in favor of a unilateral engagement: anti-industrialism of a romantically Socialistic sort; and Communists may have been just as shocked by it as capitalists.

By implicating itself with the "practical," this estheticism becomes itself assertive, almost dogmatic, in its limited antithesis. (For the first time, the editorial "we" crops up in such contexts in *Counter-Statement.*) These new aims mark the transition from the skeptical "supreme game of the mind" to something very close to pamphleteering (CS, vii). Since absolute skepticism no doubt taxes the human capability for bearing stresses to, and perhaps beyond, its limit, it is psychologically understandable that a demand for certainty asserts itself, especially in a time and an environment in which the very physical subsistence is endangered. The near-annihilation that marks the end of *The White Oxen* is but the counterpart of the almost desperate bid for a modicum of certainty in "Program" and a call for a controversial, antithetical "norm" in the final passages of *Counter-Statement*. The same crisis is still to be felt in the subsequent quest for permanence, for stability, for a "better life."

The politico-economical speculations at the end of *Counter-Statement* point to the next phase of Burke's development in still another way: they indicate his rising concern with non-literary matters. By employing and balancing primarily the perspectives of sociology, psychology, and semantics, he begins to practice his program of a skeptical syncretism. When he later returns to literary criticism, he brings to bear the results of his speculations by yet more intensive insights into certain aspects of a literary work. As his next book, however, Burke publishes a highly stylized, fascinating novel—or, perhaps more precisely, anti-novel—which has recently been reissued after more than thirty years of unjustified neglect.

CHAPTER 4

At War with Oneself

I *The Place of* Towards a Better Life *in Burke's Writing*

THERE is a striking similarity between Burke's novel of introspection, *Towards a Better Life* (1932) and his later book of speculation, *Permanence and Change* (1935). At the end of the novel, John Neal, the hero, virtually "goes to pieces." He talks to a dummy policeman, to an *alter ego,* to other projections of his paranoic mind. His discourse, long since become a monologue, disintegrates into "jottings," troubled aphorisms, obsessive images ("die as a mangled wasp dies"—note the adjective!), and finally terminates in "silence, that the torrent may be heard descending in all its fulness." [1] Similarly, *Permanence and Change* is "such a book as authors in those days [of the Great Depression] put together to keep themselves from falling apart" (PC, xiii). But in the later book, which goes beyond the earlier novel, only its first two parts furnish a parallel for the over-all development of John Neal's career. The speaker of *Permanence and Change,* Burke himself, leaves Neal behind, pulls through the crisis, and finally catches a new foothold—a new basis of a better life by looking afresh at his old convictions.

The novel foreshadows the later book both in the general pattern and in some significant points of detail. Its style, eloquence, and wit tie in with the rhetorical concerns of *Counter-Statement.* In fact, the major part of the novel was written simultaneously with the third part of *Counter-Statement;* from 1928 to 1930 its first ten chapters were serialized as consecutively numbered "Declamations" in *The Dial, The Hound and Horn,* and *Pagany* successively. *Towards a Better Life* thus documents an important phase in Burke's development, while in itself it is a distinct, excellently written, and captivating contribution to the American literature of the 1920's and 1930's.

II *The Theory behind the Novel*

To call *Towards a Better Life* a novel requires an immediate modification. For, in writing this book, Burke followed a method which reverses that of the realistic, objective, "journalistic" novel: instead of inventing a conventional plot—a chain of events from which the reader may infer the emotions and attitudes involved—he intended to render attitudes explicit, primarily the ones which he singled out as the "Six Biblical Characteristics, the Six Pivotals": "lamentation, rejoicing, beseechment, admonition, sayings, and invective" (TBL, viii–ix). From this point of view the book seems to lack what Eliot has called the "objective correlative."

In this sense, Burke violated the categorical formal expectations of the audience; neither did he draw upon conventionally effective novelistic situations. Since he thus did not make objective symbols, he found himself in the predicament of most modern writers: he faced the need to make his subjective symbols effective, as he had explained in a general discussion in *Counter-Statement* (CS, 192–97). His way of doing so was to emphasize "the essayistic rather than the narrative, the emotional predicament of [his] hero rather than the details by which he arrived at them—the ceremonious, formalized, 'declamatory'" (TBL, ix). As a result, "Mr. Burke succeed[ed] in making a pathology realistic." [2] Seen from this angle, *Towards a Better Life* does supply an objective correlative: it offers a sympathetic understanding of a process of utter mental bewilderment.

With the same perspective, one can recognize that this anti-novel implicitly also contains a genuine novel, whose contours become more and more distinct as the declamatory revelations unfold. Burke indeed minimizes circumstantial information and capitalizes upon the brilliantly selected word. But, clearly, a great part of the saliency of the narrative, and particularly of the concluding passages, depends exactly upon the set of conditions and attitudes which the reader has been able to infer from John Neal's declamations.

Because all events are presented only as reflected through this character's consciousness, *Towards a Better Life* is even directly connected with the realistic, dramatic novel of the type of *The*

Ambassadors. Both types differ, however, insofar as in Henry James's novel the artistic focus is upon the interaction between Strether's sensibility, knowledge, and judgment and the action in which he participates. The point of view is limited, but the plot is presented realistically. The personal insights and the events depicted have equal structural weight. In the story of John Neal, on the other hand, the events are totally subordinate to the central consciousness; it is hard to say where the realistic sizing-up ends and delusion begins: the whole imaginative sphere is filled with a single awareness and a single monologue.

III *The Story of John Neal*

As a heuristic device, it is helpful to reconstruct the events about which John Neal verbalizes. Yet since in Burke's novel the physical action clearly is the most ephemeral aspect, and since, furthermore, Neal, particularly in the advanced stages of his derangement, is only a very unreliable witness of his own life, this plot outline cannot be more than the first rough draft of an analysis.

So much is clear: John Neal is a *littérateur* who for the most part lives in New York City. His downfall occurs in three phases corresponding to the three parts of the book, and the time of action definitely spans a period of well over two years, probably more. He is obsessed with the fear of a great disaster and tries to steel himself for it by courting minor ones of his own making; thus, by his own devising, he puts himself on the highroad to the final catastrophe (TBL, 59). Neal is in love with Florence, an actress. Memories of these happy days are among the most beautiful passages of the book:

> With fallen branches, as dry and brittle as chalk, and some dead leaves gathered from the crevices, I made us a bedding, where we half reclined and talked. The snow still lay about in irregular patches, like the spots of sunshine that filter through the trees in midsummer. Also, a few of last year's leaves were clinging to the oaks—and it was these leaves now which began to rustle, first far off in the valley under a slow breeze which came upon us a full minute in arrears of its own sound, so that we heard this rustling in other areas while the woods about us were still quiet; thus warned, we could observe the crackling foliage pass from its

initial interrupted twitchings into a state of vigorous commotion. The crowns of the trees then yielded, each after its fashion; a few scattered pads of rain fell, visible not as drops but in the starting of dead leaves; and the woods were now beset by a miniature fury so thorough, so all-pervasive, that it even caught at the hems of our coats, suggesting to me in the general flurry the thought that I might, with mock-possessiveness, act as though shielding her in some grave onslaught. We peered studiously into the vacant forest as the breeze dropped away, and everything again became silent, leaving no echo but that in our own minds. (TBL, 27–28)

But, when his friend Anthony, an actor, begins to court Florence, Neal, while desperately loving her, does all in his power to build their happiness out of his own despair: in the end he even gives them keys to his apartment separately, thus contriving their union. Still, he continues to compete on a ground which he had strategically selected for his own defeat: since his rival is rich, he squanders his own little fortune in a pretentious show of high living. Then, destitute, he leaves for a country town which he has picked at random.

The second part of the novel relates John Neal's fortunes and misfortunes there. Characteristically, he begins by violently denouncing his fellow men *in toto*, a kind of invective which recurs in many forms in the later parts of the book. This is a pauper's way of imitating Jean des Esscintes' building of a paradisiacal refuge from society, for the wealthy French baron of J.-K. Huysmans' *A Rebours* (1883) furnished his secluded country house with all sorts of fantastic equipment to provide him with material for dreaming: a library of late Latin authors, a boudoir of exotic plants, a gallery of sadistic etchings, an "organ" of outlandish perfumes. Neal, on the other hand, constructs his psychopathic monastery by a mental transvaluation of all values so that, as Malcolm Cowley observes in his perceptive review, "the busy, complacent people about him are shown to be mentally sluggish, morally evasive; while he himself, the ingrate and smell-feast, assumes his true role as an active and courageous prophet." [3] A procedure similar to Neal's imaginary, thorough, and methodical reversal of customary perspectives later becomes Burke's systematic and explicit methodology in *Permanence and Change*.

Fortified by his mental calisthenics, Neal begins to perpetrate ignobilities upon the people closest to him. First, he finds consolation in the arms of Genevieve, a gentle and generous woman who loves him truly, despite the fact that he falsely tells her that he is married, and who also disregards his other mental cruelties. Then he dismisses her to marry another woman by whom he has children, and he becomes a local dignitary. Characteristically, his family remains faceless and nameless; for all the while Neal keeps on extending and intensifying his coercion neurosis, his self-inflicted exile from Florence, until his well-masoned mental country house becomes his dungeon.

All of a sudden, there is a promise of liberation. Neal again meets Florence, who is now touring the country with a third-rate acting company, and he shares a dingy hotel bed with her. But even this final attainment comes too late. He takes a morbid pleasure in eliciting her confessions: Anthony has sent her away; for a time, she has associated with a boxing champion; now she is completely destitute—and Neal, in his mind reproaching his former friend Anthony for the fact that he "hurried a weeping woman," does exactly the same under the guise of false promises. This chapter of his life closed, he feels his total *raison d'être* annihilated: "It was because of Florence that I had gone into this section of the country and attempted to reconstruct a new manner of living—so Florence had been primarily the force holding me here. . . . But now my conditions which I had schooled myself to cope with, were reversed. I had been pushing against a great weight—and with this weight gone, I fell forward" (TBL, 131–32).

Such impressions introduce the third and final stage of John Neal's mental decomposition. The neurosis has reached its critical point, and most of the last part of the book reads like an eloquent inside report on paranoia. There is first the classical stage of an ominous waiting for a new certainty to form itself independent, as it were, of the conscious mind of the patient. When this certainty matures, Neal stealthily leaves his family to return to New York City. Prevailing upon Genevieve, he again finds refuge with her; but he soon starts to test her fidelity in morbid ways and finally turns her away ignominiously—or is this whole episode already a fabrication of his deluded mind? Under the stress of his self-inflicted mental regimen he feels that his mind is like a "fist so tightly clenched that the whole arm tremble[s]. . . . It is as though the pulpy substance of the brain were turning into muscle, and these muscles were straining to tear apart their own tissue" (TBL, 189).

This convulsive image is both an epiphany of the last-but-one stage of Neal's breakdown and a literary memory, an adaptation and expansion of Thomas Mann's description of Gustav von Aschenbach's moral fiber—a passage which Burke had chosen as the representative anecdote of an earlier essay.[4] In this way, Neal's life is squeezed farther and farther into the narrow end of a funnel (TBL, 191). Cut off from all normal contact, he accosts strangers in the park, he is obsessed with symbols of division, he converses with an *alter ego,* he refers to himself in the third person. Hopelessly enmeshed in a mental cocoon of his own making, John Neal comes to a Nietzschean end; his monologue subsides into the silence of insanity.

IV *The Title*

How can such a career as that of John Neal be a development "towards a better life"? Certainly, irony figures high in the choice of the title. But there is more to it. In the first place, the title phrase, which in its very wording manifests a transitoriness which Burke was later to note in the prepositional titles of the novels of Huysmans' period of "rebirth," titles such as *A Rebours, En Route, Là-Bas* (ATH, 64), is a quotation from the text: significantly, it refers to a plan of the antagonist. It is Anthony who, as Neal relates, uses this phrase to describe his project of founding an apparently utopian colony. Neal then employs the same expression to accuse Anthony of facile idealism and opportunism, and he later accuses him of rigging the whole project only as a strategy, a subterfuge to gain the attention, interest, and love of Florence (TBL, 58–59, 110). Thus, the title refers only indirectly to Neal's life; it may be taken to apply somewhat more directly to Burke's own career in the sense that his fictitious account of a mental breakdown may have helped him by providing a negative example.

V *Second-Person Singular*[5]

The technique for rendering this record of a psychopath's career so very effective is, apart from the eloquent language and the skillful pacing of the narrative, the device of feigned address, maintained throughout. Officially, the chapters are undated, unsent letters to Anthony, Neal's friend and rival; one late chapter consists of a fiction within the fiction: it contains unsent letters to Genevieve, presented as "A Story by John Neal."

But there is more to the I/you relationship in *Towards a Better Life*. Just as with T. S. Eliot's *The Waste Land,* a poem which Burke had repeatedly commented upon, much of the novel's structure and meaning can be disclosed by a closer analysis of the ways in which the different pronouns interact. For in the use of the second-person singular in this book there is also a sizable amount of a direct address to the reader which moves from invective to beseechment. In back of Anthony, as it were, the reader finds himself as a *dramatis persona,* and the narrator tries to hold him by the sheer power of his address, much as the Ancient Mariner held the wedding guest. There are also many instances in which the reader is incorporated into the crowd collectively inveighed against.

Yet the I/you relationship becomes significant even at a more submerged level: "Let us go, then, you and I . . ."—the technique of the introspective dialogue employed, for instance, in Eliot's *Prufrock*, is also operative in *Towards a Better Life*. Not only does John Neal, in the end, discourse extensively with a projected *alter ego;* there are prior references to projection as a scapegoat mechanism (esp. TBL, 78); and even such early passages as the following intimate a psychic split: "We would not deny the mind; but merely remember that as the corrective of wrong thinking is right thinking, the corrective of all thinking is the body./You moralistic dog—admitting a hierarchy in which you are subordinate, purely that you may have subordinates . . ." (TBL, 9).

Who is the butt of this invective? Anthony?—certainly. The reader?—possibly. But apart from them, he is a part of the narrator's own self. On this level, *Towards a Better Life* can be read as a *roman à clef,* a key to Burke's mind at that time.[6] Burke later recurs again and again to the idea of the multiple personality: "The so-called 'I' is merely a unique combination of partially conflicting 'corporate we's' " (ATH, 264). He later bases his analysis of literature as ritual, as symbolic action, upon the assumption that the split personality is the rule (ATH, 184). Thus, taking the cue from the close juxtaposition of "body" and "you" in the above quotation, it is arguable that, in passages like this one, "you" addresses the somatic subpersonality, "I" speaks for the mental one, and "we" subsumes both as the master personality. But one should not think that Anthony and Neal, throughout, are allegorical figures of body and mind, respectively; nevertheless, there is certainly a sense in which they are impersonations of Gudruff and Prince Llan from the final *White Oxen* story.

When, toward the end of the novel, the narrator recommends, "Watch the mind, as you would eye a mean dog" (TBL, 208), it is important to note that the speaker is no longer John Neal but one who has left him behind. For the narrator of these final passages consistently refers to Neal in the *third* person singular (TBL, 203–8). Psychologically, such a self-alienation is a classical symptom of an advanced stage of paranoia; esthetically, this technique expresses an advance in point of view. Burke surmounts what he has experienced as the self-destructive element of the purely subjective intellect. As Cowley sees it, the moral implied in *Towards a Better Life* is: "There is no salvation apart from society." [7]

In terms of the history of fiction, Burke's novel intensifies traits implicit in Symbolist novels such as Huysmans'; there are not only similarities of sensibility and structure but even of detail. It also radicalizes James's technique of the central intelligence. Furthermore, it has justly been compared with Virginia Woolf's novels, especially with *The Waves*.[8] And it certainly did its share to make possible such later experimental novels as Djuna Barnes's *Nightwood* (1936). For a comparison of Miss Barnes's novel and Burke's it is an important clue that Eliot's introduction to *Nightwood*, with its emphasis on a "written" style and its avoidance of the "noises" of daily communication, reads much like the preface to *Towards a Better Life*.[9] Burke's novel is unique among these others insofar as it pushes the subjective, monological approach to its extreme and does not incorporate any reliable objective narration whatsoever. Furthermore, not until the recent French *anti-roman,* not until Michel Butor's *Paris-Rome, ou la Modification*

(1957), has the device of a feigned audience address been used in such a structurally prominent way.

In terms of Kenneth Burke's own career, the outcome of his novel explains much of the slant of his next books. He fell forward, when the weight was gone. After he had imaginatively tracked down the extreme dissociative possibilities of a single-minded intellectual and psychic subjectivism—what wonder that he later overrates communication, community, and communism?

CHAPTER 5

Vision and Revision

I *Burke's Books of the 1930's*

PERMANENCE *and Change* (1935), *Attitudes toward History* (1937), and *The Philosophy of Literary Form* (1941) are closely interrelated. The last one, despite its publishing date, is really a book of the 1930's; for it is composed of critical essays and reviews written between 1933 and 1940. *Permanence and Change* and the previously unpublished title essay of *The Philosophy of Literary Form* constitute the two foci of this phase of Burke's work. *Permanence and Change* develops a system of thought based on an amazing wealth of sociological, psychological, economic, semantic, historical, anthropological, and other studies, synthetized in an imaginative world view called Metabiology. *The Philosophy of Literary Form* employs all this material to devise a method of acute exegesis of all kinds of literary texts as rituals symbolic of their authors' engrossments.

In this scheme, *Attitudes toward History* serves almost as a set of emancipated footnotes to *Permanence and Change*. For, in Part III of *Attitudes toward History*, Burke again followed his inclination toward lexicological exposition by writing an alphabetized "Dictionary of Pivotal Terms," a precise and concise statement of the views on art and life which he then held. In Part II, "The Curve of History," Burke presents Western history as a five-act drama; and in this way he restates the metaphysical speculations of *Permanence and Change* in historical terms; but he also goes beyond the poetic communism, with which he culminated the earlier book, by recommending a "comic frame," a post-ideological attitude of irony that somewhat resembles his early antithetical estheticism. A section of Part I of *Attitudes toward History* is important as a document of his indebtedness to William James's moralistic voluntarism, the "will to believe" (cf. also PC, 236). In the remaining portions of the book, particularly "Poetic Categories" and the extended essay on "Ritual," Burke takes up problems of literary theory as they grow out of his comprehensive world view; and in this way he foreshadows the solutions found in *The Philosophy of Literary Form.*

In this context, *Permanence and Change* serves as Burke's central "Vision" to which he was to return again and again both for inspiration and for revision. The subsequent discussion concentrates on an exposition of the main enduring elements and one or two instances of revision, and treats them in relative isolation; the following preliminary general characterization of the book's overall pattern is designed as a first approximation.

II *Perspectivist Readings of a Study in Perspectivism*

Permanence and Change has been read as a textbook in social psychology, and it has also been emphatically recommended as a guide to the "sociological imagination" by so eminent a sociologist as C. Wright Mills.[1] By the same criterion, other reviewers, among them the no less reputed critic, Austin Warren, have complained about the book's defective structure—its lack of direction.[2] As it stands, *Permanence and Change* offers the opportunity to follow a speculative thinker on the arduous but pleasurable journey of his thought *as it becomes articulate.* It imitates thought processes in action, with the inevitable digressions, regressions, recapitulations, contradictions, and corrections.

This mode of exposition could be described as "stream-of-consciousness at one remove," heading toward rhetorical organization. No doubt it was with this quality in mind that reviewers referred to the book as a "poet's work, lyric, intuitive, satiric," a "pre-poem," and "another self-contradictory expression of the . . . modern madness."[3] In this sense, *Permanence and Change,* written in 1932–33 (CS, 216), could be read as a speculative expression of anguish at the modern transvaluation of values, intensified by the economic hazards of the Great Depression.

Another valid approach would be to read the book as a philosophical exploration of the poetry/science alignment around which *Counter-Statement* was constructed—but with "magic" and "religion" as additional key terms. Or, to follow Burke's own lead, one could analyze it as built around the "purely imaginal process" of the tripartite rebirth ritual (CS, 215). In this way, the book's structure would come close to the tragic rhythm of action (cf. below, Chapter 8, Section II b), whose three stages—purpose, reversal by passion, and perception (or new purpose)—are indeed parallel to the three parts of *Permanence and Change*. "On Interpretation" explores how an orientation takes form and reluctantly finds its representative anecdote in behavioristic experiments which show that infants arbitrarily and irrationally—but methodically—associate experiences by *transference*. The middle part, "Perspective by Incongruity," develops a method of inference on this basis; and the concluding "Basis of Simplification" uses all the previous considerations to devise the world view of Metabiology, a philosophy of being which states principles that, according to Burke, underly all "becoming," all historical change.

One important qualification must, however, be made when looking at the book as rebirth ritual: although the method of "perspective by incongruity" is analogically described as "verbal 'atom cracking' " (ATH, 308), and although the subject matter of the middle part therefore resembles the most acute kind of "passion," namely the *sparagmos* (the rending apart of the sacrificial figure in the fertility rites on which the tragic rhythm of action is modeled), the *reversal*, or rebirth, is not at all complete. This incompleteness is documented by the fact that the central method and such key terms as "linkage," "trained incapacity," and "occupational psychosis" are carried over intact from the first into the third part of the book. Since, therefore, the third or "perception" part emerges only with a partially new insight, the symbolic pattern of *Permanence and Change* is rather that of a violent intensification of mental anguish, which is checked in the end. The symbolic action underlying and motivating the public purpose of the book is a personal ritual of accepting perspectives which previously were at least half rejected.

III *Magic: An Example of Revision*

The most important perspective which Burke persuades himself to assume is a post-scientific orientation envisaged at the end of Part I and developed in Part III. He offers it as the culmination of the "three [previous successive] orders of rationalization" (or orientation; PC, 59–66): magic, the control of "natural forces"; religion, of "human forces"; and science, of the "third productive order, the technological." [4] As Burke sees it, this technological orientation permeates all contemporary thought and behavior (PC, 44), even language. For the neutral, conceptual style of exposition that has been developed by insisting on fixed definitions is, in his opinion, an idiom "designed for machines" (PC, 58). And he feels that it is necessary to go beyond this "technological psychosis" because science and the "scientific" language in many ways violate human needs. In Burke's view, science is overly exploiting and combative (PC, 172–73); it has contributed decisively to the modern dissociation of thought and feeling (PC, 176); and, strangely enough, he regards science as too individualistic (PC, 101). By contrast, the scheme of orientation which he sets out to propagate is cooperative, poetic, "anthropomorphic and humanistic," communal, even Communistic.[5] But the communism which Burke recommends is of an idealistic, tentative kind; and, though there are many references to Marx, the principles of a philosophy of *being* definitely carry Burke beyond any shade of orthodox Marxism.

In developing this quaternary scheme—magic, religion, science, poetry—Burke encounters difficulties, primarily with regard to his concept of magic. He derives it from Frazer who, he says, identifies magic with science as the two coercive attitudes of man toward his environment; both presuppose a universe which can be manipulated at will when its immutable laws have been mastered (PC, 59–60). To these two orientations, Burke opposes religion and, implicitly at this point, poetry; they represent the propitiatory principle and postulate an ethical, ever-creative universe based on choice. In establishing this alignment, Burke overrides distinctions between magic and science which Frazer recognized, despite the similarities, when he speaks in *The Golden Bough* of the "mistaken application" of scientific principles in magic, when he calls its claims "false." [6] *Per contra,* Burke holds that magic was "on the whole astonishingly successful" (PC, 61); for it managed to secure the survival of the people under its sway and always contained realistic ingredients, such as sowing in a fertility rite.

This argument involves Burke in a tangle of unnecessary difficulties. In the first place, the philosophy of *being* at which *Permanence and Change* aims (PC, 163), and which he envisages as a *poetic* orientation, especially in the form of his later Dramatistic speculations concerning the immutable grounds of human action, confusingly vows him—to make a provisionary use of his own distinctions—to *magical-scientific* (not "poetic") pursuits, to the exploration of eternal laws. But, paradoxically, even in *Permanence and Change* Burke soon begins to re-align magic with poetry (PC, 72–77). Especially his review of Jeremy Bentham's semantic analyses forces him to do so: accordingly, every single speech-act is necessarily poetic, suggestive, magical, insofar as it conveys the attitudes of the speaker; and, given an ideal community, it coerces (perhaps only induces?) the audience to react correspondingly (PC, 177, *passim*).

Burke could have avoided this quandary about the exact place of magic in his scheme had he recognized that the correctness of magic depends on the extent to which it contains science, and had he then seen that what remains as pure magic is indeed straightforward manipulation of the audience. For, to give an example, magically to "sing the sun up" is in no way to coerce *nature;* rather, the magician is completely controlled by the laws of the universe; and, exploiting his superior knowledge of the situation, he plays upon a credulous *audience's* psychology, much as Burke's poet plays upon the audience ideology in an ideal community. About fifteen years later, Burke is much closer to the mark when he distinguishes between two brands of magic, "bad science" and "primitive rhetoric" [7]; but there is a sense in which magic is bad science exactly because it is rhetorically effective. Recently, Burke has completely rectified his early error when he defined magic as "good rhetoric," as the means for "bringing about the inevitable" (LSA, 396).

IV *Elements of Permanence*

Apart from such views as that of magic which required revision, *Permanence and Change* contains many elements which Burke retained as cornerstones of his later work. There is, for instance, a striking theory of history. In its expanded form as presented in *Attitudes toward History*, it has received isolated high praise[8]; but it was, on the whole, disregarded. Like all other speculations in *Permanence and Change*, this theory is based on the assumption that man's "organic genius," his psychosomatic structure, is the "rock-bottom" of certitude because it "exists prior to any historical texture" (PC, 226). The historical changes, then, are motivated by the fact that the predominating orientation of a given period emphasizes certain aspects of this universal nature of man and thwarts others, a frustration which requires a reorientation by which "the faulty emphases of [the] day may be rectified" (PC, 182). The new set of attitudes gradually extends and finally becomes so entrenched that it demands a new adjustment: Burke proposes what could be called "dialectical biologism."

Another enduring contribution made in the book is a general theory of psychotherapy. According to it, analytic treatment is effective because by "secular conversion (downward)" the analyst progressively misnames a patient's syndrome in the most incongruous and innocuous, that is, regressive, infantile terms. Sometimes such an "exorcism by misnomer" (PC, 142), which systematically razes the neurotic associations that have coercively been constructed on the basis of the original traumatic experience, is sufficient per se. But, even if this cure in terms of the *id* does not work in itself, it clears the ground for a less idiosyncratic and more adequate reorientation. This second phase, the cure in terms of the *superego,* rebuilds the patient's personality by "socializing [his] new mental structure by anchoring it to an obvious feature of the *group psychosis*" (PC, 132). (It must be added that Burke here uses the term "psychosis" not in the psychoanalytical sense, but in keeping with Dewey's formula "occupational psychosis" as a synonym for "orientation"; "rationalization," used non-pejoratively, is another frequent Burkean equivalent.)

The most important part of *Permanence and Change* expounds Burke's theory of intellection, "perspective by incongruity." It is the basis of all the other theories. Like them, it is derived from the book's representative anecdote, the behavioristic theory of learning by transference.

V *Transference, Linkage, Merger, Cluster-Formation, Identification*

As John B. Watson's experiments have shown, infants transfer to rabbits their reactions of fear provoked by the violent clanging of iron bars, if they are shown rabbits simultaneously with the din. What is more, they will, to a lesser degree, even make secondary transferences from rabbits to furs and will react fearfully to the "rabbitness of fur coats" (PC, 11–13). Burke uses these behaviorist experiments in the transference of the conditioned reflex, or "linkage," as he calls this mechanism of identification, to obliterate the difference between reasoning and *post factum* rationalization by claiming that every orientation or training is a specific way of establishing such compulsive linkages. A set or cluster of such linkages or mergers becomes a unit in a person's world view: it characterizes his "occupational psychosis." This view is the basis of Burke's later theory of literature.

An occupation (or pre-occupation) is a self-perpetuating system; it "creates" the interpretation of new situations. Conversely, the very *capacities* which a person acquires through *training incapacitate* him for *other* activities. A good way of visualizing such a "trained incapacity" (Veblen's term) is to think of a sailor's gait when he walks on dry land, and then to extend this principle to other "walks of life."

VI *Perspective by Incongruity*[9]

The preceding considerations contain the basic elements for an understanding of Burke's central speculative technique—perspective by incongruity. In fact, the example involving the sailor, with its metaphorical extension of the word "walk" is a minor, mild instance of such a perspective: it serves to bring out a new insight —or, at least, to make a dormant one salient. Formally defined, a perspective by incongruity works by "violating the 'proprieties' of [a] word in its previous linkages" (PC, 90). In this sense, it is "impious," or controversial, because it is the verbal expression of an act of transvaluation of received values. Thus, for example, the slogan "Support our boys in Vietnam" piously states an orthodox patriotic verity; adding the phrase "Bring them home" amounts to a shattering of this conventional view by a redefinition of the meaning of "support" and the consequent assertion of the superiority of the individual's welfare over his nation's commitments.

Burke, on his part, credits his inspiration for the intellective method of perspective by incongruity to Nietzsche's argumentative maneuvers in *The Will to Power* (PC, 88); and he also finds it manifest in the work of the philosophers and scientists who have influenced Burke most: Spengler, Darwin, Bergson, Marx, Freud; the names of Frazer and de Gourmont could be added to this list. Spengler's cyclical theory of history, for instance, is based on the redefinition of the term "contemporaneity" and identifies *corresponding* phases of *subsequent* cultures as contemporaneous; thus, for instance, he speaks of "Arabic Puritanism" (PC, 89). Similarly, Marx's concept and program of the class consciousness of the international proletariat establishes a perspective by incongruity by impiously cutting across national alignments (PC, 113). Darwin performed perhaps the most radical perspective by incongruity by the "transference of man from the category of the divine to the category of the apes" (PC, 73). Burke, following Bergson—who postulated that the rigid classificatory system of language is unable to make realistic predications about a world of absolute flux except by paradoxical propositions (PC, 92–94)—concentrates on the cultivation of "planned incongruity" as an epistemological device. He aims at the "bureaucratization," the " 'mass production' of perspectives." His methodology, he claims, "*makes perspectives cheap and easy*" (ATH, 228–29). What, then, is the actual technique of forcing a perspective by incongruity?

VII *Terminological Collage, Analogical Extension, Rational Pun*

Planned incongruity could be sloganized as "a progression from fashion through fission to fusion." It can formally be analyzed as a two-part process: its first phase, from fashion to fission, is identical with de Gourmont's dissociation of received ideas, of views which are fashionable. Its second phase, from fission to fusion, aims at the reintegration of the dissociated elements to form a new orientation by the "methodic merger of particles that had been considered mutually exclusive" (PC, xxi). The whole process of planned incongruity is motivated by a given occupational or pre-occupational interest (PC, 107). Grotesque figures, Joyce's "linguistic gargoyles," caricatures, and Surrealist paintings are among its manifestations (PC, 112–13). Specifically, Burke recommends the following procedures:

> Let us not only discuss a nation as though it were an individual, but also an individual as though he were a nation, depicting massive events trivially, and altering the scale of weeds in a photograph until they become a sublime and towering forest—

> shifting from the animal, the vegetable, the physical, the mental, "irresponsibly" applying to one category the terms habitual to another, as when Whitehead discerns mere habit in the laws of atomic behavior—or like a kind of Professorial E. E. Cummings who, had he called man an ape, would then study apes to understand Aristotle. "Let us do this?" Everywhere, in our systems for forcing inferences, it is being done. (PC, 122)

All these examples and recommendations again point in one direction: toward *collage,* collage without glue.[10] This speculative process is parallel to the most characteristic of Burke's fictional techniques. It could be defined as collage of ideas, or, perhaps more correctly, as *terminological* collage. Burke actually calls it "analogical extension," in keeping with his recommendation to carry over terms from one category into another. He equates this process with metaphor (ATH, 230) and the *rational,* not the *tonal,* pun or double meaning (ATH, 309)—though he also likes to draw upon tonal puns. As one example of such an analogical extension one might cite Burke's belief that art is the most sensitive dial for the recording of all fundamental psychological processes because the artist intuitively feels and expresses the slightest cultural changes. Accordingly, the " 'poetry exchange' is to human living as a whole what the stock exchange is to production and distribution under capitalism" (ATH, 202). This statement has the proportional form of an analogy. The term "exchange" is metaphorically extended from the commercial to the esthetic terminology and thus assumes an unusual double meaning. Being admonished by Burke to look for the occupational interest behind such a strategy, one can distinguish a poet's endeavor to bestow dignity and importance upon his trade by borrowing a term from an activity which commands a wide interest and a great reputation in his society.

There is no doubt that "planned incongruity" makes for effective, memorable statements. Metaphor certainly figures high among the devices of power of expression. But a legitimate and effective poetic and rhetorical device need not always serve as a workable means of forcing inferences. The epistemological problems involved are delicate and complex. So much is certain: even if real, revolutionary insights require terminological collages for their verbal expression, it does not follow that the reversal of the process, the mass production of verbal incongruities, necessarily and in all cases leads to valid insights. If this methodology "makes insights cheap and easy," may it not, on occasions, easily cheapen them?

This reflection raises another point, also not for settlement in this context, but for consideration: Burke is aware of the fact that arguments by analogy easily lend themselves to mystification. Thus, in the Middle Ages it was held that there should be two authorities in the world, the pope and the emperor, and that the latter should receive his power from the former, just as there are two "authorities" in the celestial world, the sun and the moon, with the latter receiving its light from the former. Apart from the fact that the relationship between celestial bodies and human functionaries is tenuous, the analogy could just as well be reversed to promote the cause of imperial supremacy over the papacy. It all depends on the point of view of him who uses this analogy. Because of the danger of such anthropomorphic rationalizations, analogy has come in for Kantian criticism as an improper, over-stretching device of theological and metaphysical speculation.

Burke would meet such an objection by the just claim that it is impossible to devise a wholly non-metaphorical, non-analogical terminology (ATH, 311), which he would prefer (ATH, 232). Therefore, he proposes the method of planned incongruity to "channelize an evil" which, he feels, cannot be eradicated (ATH, 236). In his view, the difference between mystification and clarification lies in the fact that the first *conceals* the strategy; the latter *reveals* it (ATH, 232).[11] By "revealing," Burke does not mean to discover and discount the element of mystification in somebody else's discourse and to avoid it as far as possible in one's own discursive writings—a use to which his perceptive analyses are exceptionally well adapted—but to analyze the method of this strategy and to employ it systematically. It is impossible to do completely without metaphor. But is deliberate and methodological mystification really superior to a consistent and unconscious practice? To the extent that Burke uses these devices in all of his writings, even his criticism and philosophy tend toward myth or poetry.[12]

It would seem that reasoning by analogy can serve not to force inferences but to devise working hypotheses and to reaffirm opinions for an audience that is already convinced. Terminological collage has its value as a presentational device and as a heuristic method, subject to verification. Verification, as Burke sees it, operates through "recalcitrance"—the strategic alteration of one's arguments when they meet with opposition, their modification for the purpose of communicating one's vision (PC, 256–58); the "nature of the world itself" appears as mediated through rhetoric. For instance, a planned incongruity, *verbally* in strict agreement with Darwin's findings, could transfer man into the category not of the apes but the ants. Burke considers this possibility in *The Philosophy of Literary Form,* but he finally opts for an alternative, man as communicant. His method of verification, of assessing recalcitrance, is the dialectical process of exploring the "scope, range, relevancy, accuracy, and applicability of the perspective" (PLF, 127). This admission of some kind of principle of validation is an advance over the largely uncontrolled perspectivism of *Permanence and Change.*

While the above considerations are presented in a tentative spirit and also indicate some later revisions made by Burke, there is one respect in which his concept of analogy is inadequate. For, though he warns the reader not to mistake similarity for identity (PC, 97), many of his arguments concentrate on similarity to the exclusion of dissimilarity—on a procedure of "essentializing" which actually amounts to identification. For example, there are real and important differences between Marxism and capitalism; both systems propose virtually opposite means of socio-economic control. Yet from the bio-mystical perspective of D. H. Lawrence, Burke asserts, "capitalist and Marxist would merge, since both factions accept industrial values which Lawrence would contemn" (PC, 224). In this context, it is important to note that Burke's own world view, in which *Permanence and Change* culminates, is to a large extent based on a "qualified defense" of Lawrence's views (PC, 250–55). Burke at this point endorses Lawrence's oversimplifying "essentializing" perspective.

Burke recognizes but embraces the element of "stupidity" or "bluntness" implied in such a perspectivism (PC, 106, 124–25) which gives up previous insights with each shift of angle. Yet is there not a rational way for overcoming the stultification of the rationalizing Laurentian perspective? One would have to recognize the differences on top of the common industrial orientation of Marxism and capitalism, and specifically account for them, while acknowledging the common traits. Only by taking both the real similarities *and* the real differences fully into account is it possible to go beyond the anarchy of shifting perspectives which would, after all, be irrelevant because each shift methodically sacrifices insights gained by the previous orientation.

Burke's concept of analogy is not fully equipped for this realistic sizing-up because it slights *differentiae*.[13] It is clearly modeled upon the behavioristic experiments in the undiscriminating transference of the conditioned reflex. Such a "linkage" may be natural for infants and also for adults in situations of tension and terror. The fact that Burke so heavily relies on the automatism of psychological transference in devising the world view of *Permanence and Change* can serve as an indicator of the amount and intensity of stress and intellectual anguish under which the book was written.

The briefest possible formula for summing up the jist of *Permanence and Change* is perhaps to note that it is built around the words "communication," "communicant," and "communism" (of an idealistic, unorthodox type) to indicate the interrelationship of esthetic-linguistic, magical-religious, and socio-political processes.[14] Rephrased in psychoanalytical terms, this observation amounts to saying that in this book Burke explores the *id*'s fantastic resources and the societal restraint imposed upon it by the *superego*, omitting, to a great extent, considerations of the resultant development of the *ego*. Or, still more concisely, *Permanence and Change* could be described as the expression of the "occupational psychosis" of a poet engrossed in reorientation, as a radical application of Nietzsche's theorem according to which art is the last metaphysical resort in an era of nihilism.

CHAPTER 6

Verbalization as Attitude

As a first step toward an understanding of Burke's theory of poetry as symbolic action, which emerges from the general concerns of *Permanence and Change,* it is necessary to give an account of the way his concept of poetry was transformed when it was placed into the wide circumference of the metabiological world view. The consequent changes of, and additions to, the analytical tools of *Counter-Statement* are made in a preliminary way in several sections of *Attitudes toward History:* in "Poetic Categories," "General Nature of Ritual," and in most entries of the "Dictionary of Pivotal Terms." It is the next book, *The Philosophy of Literary Form,* that presents the new literary theory fully and systematically. This poetic was not substantially modified—only supplemented—later when Burke placed it into the still wider context of Dramatism, which, in turn, emerged from it. It constitutes Burke's most significant contribution to literary theory, and consequently it merits extensive discussion and careful examination in the third and major part of this chapter. In the short second part the transitional stage of *Attitudes toward History* is summarized, and this summary serves as an indicator of the changes resulting from the universal "poetic" of *Permanence and Change,* which is discussed next.

I *The Poetic of* Permanence and Change

The poetic of *Permanence and Change* is an extension of Burke's theory of language as censorial (as expressive of the speaker's attitude) and as essentially communicative (depending on the community's ideology) and, finally, of his teleological Metabiology. The variable meaning of the key terms, "poetry," "style," and "symbol," are indicative of this orientation. In *Permanence and Change,* "poetry" first emerges as the corrective to "science" (PC, 65–66); but, in continuance of the trend toward widening the context of esthetic speculation, begun in the third phase of *Counter-Statement* ("Program"), the all-pervasive *metaphysical* function which is attributed to poetry at the end of *Permanence and Change* is already intimated in the beginning of the book. Later, in connection with references to Jeremy Bentham's analyses of speech, "poetry (a *poor* brand of poetry)" becomes identified with the censorial, emotive, "magic" function of words in general (PC, 75, 177).

From this association it is only one step of "analogical extension" to claim that any person's preoccupational orientation, or "psychosis," insofar as it is a methodically constructed and piously cherished system of assertions, is a "poem" (PC, 76, 129, 153), although a bad one (PC, 158). Previously, this claim had fictitiously been made without such a qualification (TBL, 66). It also follows from the Benthamite considerations of the conditions of verbal magic in general that a poet "communicate[s] when he establishe[s] a moral identity with his group by using the same moral weightings as they use" (PC, 177–78; this view had been expressed before in a derogatory way in TBL, 86). A huge cluster of linkages is in the making: "poetry" as moral, weighted, cooperative, communistic (PC, 178)—as propaganda and partisanship (PC, 210).

Burke at this point leans toward the "agitprop" view of art as a weapon in the class struggle; but, though he always conceived of it as an "equipment for living" (PLF, 51, 253–62), the concept of art as a tool for working upon the "social reality" is, in his view of the ulterior function of poetry, overshadowed by the notion that it provides consolation and serves as a protection, primarily by "enrolling [the poet] in a band" (PLF, 32) and by the purely symbolic formation of attitudes toward the pressure of the historical texture (PLF, 269). Sometimes, as in *Permanence and Change*, Burke overstresses this point: poetry, he says, is cooperative insofar as it pleases partisans; beyond the ranks of the party, it must become an offense, a nuisance.

Style can help to widen the circle of partisans. In its "simplest manifestation, style is ingratiation," the art of "saying the right thing" (PC, 50), of "wheedling" and "cajoling." [1] How to pacify an ebullient drunk into "maudlin good-fellowship" is style (PC, 50). To be sure, Burke here talks about the simplest manifestations of style; but he does not exemplify more complex ones. Where could an analogical extension of this concept lead, after all? There is a short relative distance between the definition of esthetic truth as the exercise of human propriety in *Counter-Statement* and the coaxing of soaks.

The ultimate extension of "poetry" is reached when Burke revises Richards' distinction between statements and pseudo-statements on which *Principles of Literary Criticism* is founded. Richards had claimed that statements in poems need not have the validity of scientific predications to serve as psychotherapeutic stimuli for the author and, by proxy, for the reader.[2] In keeping with his inverted Benthamite emphasis on the magic element contained in all words, Burke points out that there can be a "pseudo" element in the most utilitarian verbalizations and actions (PC 71–72, 233–54)—as when a commodity takes on the character of a status symbol. All action is poetic insofar as it is the *symbolic* replica of the actor's personal character: "Rockefeller's economic empire is as truly a symbolic replica of his personal character as Milton's epic was a symbolic replica of Milton. In both cases the men 'socialized' their specific patterns of interest by the manipulation of objective materials in a way whereby the internal and the external were indeterminately fused" (PC, 215).

Of course, a successful "socialization" of a writer's preoccupation (his "burden," in Burke's terminology—but also his "pride"?) "must include areas of symbolization not at all local to himself" (PC, 245)—which is another way of defining recalcitrance (resistance on the part of the audience and of reality). Ultimately, all action is poetic, esthetic, ethical (PC, 215, 281, 250). All extremes coincide in a secular mysticism, a Romantic pan-estheticism: "Life itself is a poem in the sense that, in the course of living, we gradually erect a structure of relationships about us in conformity with our interests" (PC, 254). In *Attitudes toward History,* ideologies and their institutions become "'collective poems,' the total frame of thought and action" (ATH, 99).

Permanence and Change virtually eradicates the symbol/form dialectic which had characterized the esthetic of *Counter-Statement* and thus, in keeping with Burke's essentially pragmatist outlook, postulates a continuity between artistic and non-artistic intellectual activities, with only a shift of emphasis as the sole criterion of differentiation:[3] esthetic "socialization" need perhaps take only the social aspect of recalcitrance (audience resistance) into account, other "socializations" probably also physical facts. In *Permanence and Change,* Burke does not elaborate this point, but in the next book he usually discusses recalcitrance in a social or collective context (ATH, 165n, 172). In this way he views all activity in terms of an essentially symbolic core, as a spontaneous expression of the actor's interests, attitudes, preoccupations, bias. He therefore asserts the need of a "science of symbolism." In an "attempt to utilize all past frames of thought, regardless of their apparent divergencies from us," Burke calls for a

> science of symbolism as it extends all the way from new and sharper rigors of lexicography, through the various schemes of individual and group psychoanalysis (as writers like Bentham, Marx, Freud, Jung, and Burrow sought various devices for disclosing how the factor of interest bears upon our orientation) through the many attempts to found a language divorced from common sense (as with the adherents of symbolic logic, or Bergson's planned incongruity) to methodological speculations (mainly in physics and semeiotic) which lead one close to the edges of a mysticism as arrant as that of any "disorganized" medieval seer. (PC, 118)

The program for Burke's later work is now set.

II *The Transitional Stage of* Attitudes toward History

In *Counter-Statement,* the key definition of art reads: "Art enters when [a] revelation [a personal insight, a belief] is ritualized, when it is converted into a symbolic process" (CS, 168; cf. above, Chapter 3, Section VII k). The transformation characteristic of the emergent new theory could best be demonstrated by superimposing later accretions of meaning upon this key sentence. To summarize the matter in three theses: (a) the range of application widens from art to all verbalization; (b) the meaning of ritual, technique, craft diverges from audience considerations and turns toward "internal adjustments" (ATH, 200), toward the "filling out" of a perspective;[4] and (c) as a concomitant, the technical or ritualistic aspect of a work deflects from audience psychology to author psychology.

In a formulaic way, the stages of this development of Burke's literary theory can be indicated by the following sequence of phrases which are either Burke's or were coined in close adherence to his terminology:

"*verbalization* of experience" (CS, early stage)
"ramification of the symbol" (CS, middle stage)
(i.e. systematization of revelation)
ritualization of revelation (CS, final stage)
socialization of a preoccupation (PC)
"bureaucratization of the imaginative" (ATH)

All of these formulas describe essentially the same phenomenon, but the dissimilarities of implications are all-important. In order to fit the new stage of Burke's thought, the above definition of art ("Art enters . . .") would have to be revised somewhat as follows: a statement has achieved its artistically perfect form when a temperamental vision has been so thoroughly spun out that all its implications of detail have been rendered explicit, and that each and every one of its metaphors and images reflects a facet of the speaker's attitude. Works of art yield the most complex and mature insights when exposed to an analysis which takes these elements into account, because such works are characterized by a "high degree of articulateness" (PLF, 308).

In *The Tangled Bank* (1962), Stanley Edgar Hyman shows that Burke's method of symbolic analysis can be impressively adapted to the study of the imaginative strand in writings conventionally regarded as discursive or scientific. For, apart from fact, they do incorporate vision—a "symbolic synthesis" of ideas, values, images (ATH, 179). "For various reasons, one has many disparate moods and attitudes. These may be called sub-identities, sub-personalities, 'voices.' And the poet seeks to build the symbolic superstructures that put them together into a comprehensive 'super-personality'" (ATH, 184).

This ritualistic integration works by symbolic mergers, which can in turn be analyzed by examining *image clusters*. Image cluster analysis becomes an important but not exclusive method of Burke's "analytic exegesis" (ATH, 194), emerging as it does from a varied range of prior preoccupations. Remy de Gourmont's dissociation of ideas is just as manifest in it as Burke's own speculations on the possible use of concordances in the examination of the connotations of the words as a given poet uses them. Then came Caroline Spurgeon's *Shakespeare's Imagery* (1935), a book for which Burke has only the highest praise (ATH, 45–46, 273–76). He makes the best use of it that can perhaps be made by disregarding the shortcuts which Miss Spurgeon takes between Shakespeare the maker of images and plays, and Shakespeare the man: Burke draws strictly and exclusively upon her method of charting and compiling image clusters. Another influence is Bentham's theory of language and his method of metaphorical analysis; so is Ogden-Richards' view of the two uses of language, specifically the emotive one. And, not to be overlooked, there is, of course, Freud's associational method, his analysis of the pun, and other psychoanalytical devices that permeate the whole Burkean approach to literature—though Burke's theory of the psychology of the symbolic act goes beyond Freudianism and the other predecessors in quite significant ways.

III *The Psychology of the Symbolic Act*

Two kinds of inquiry are implicit in any perspective: (1) what to look for, and why; and (2) how, when, and where to look for it (PLF, 68). The present systematic discussion of Burke's analysis of symbolic action follows this scheme by first presenting the theory and then proceeding to an illustration of the practice, or methodology. The theoretical part is best discussed along four lines: (a) a sketch of its relationship to psychoanalysis; (b) an investigation of the interrelationships of the three master terms: "dream," "prayer," and "chart"; (c) an examination of the terms "situation" and "strategy"; and (d) an exposition of the symbolic act as ritual.

(a) *When psychoanalysis moves into the esthetic field.* While Freudianism is only one of the theories from which Burke derived his symbolic analysis, it may be used as a starting point of this discussion in order to bring out the important differences; for Burke has frequently been regarded as a critic who does nothing but put a poem on the analyst's couch. Yet in his essay, "Freud—and the Analysis of Poetry" (1939; PLF, 258–92), Burke notes both the similarities and the dissimilarities between the psychoanalysis of neurotics and the symbolic analysis of literary works, or poems, including "any work of critical or imaginative cast" (PLF, 1). They are similar because both the acts of the neurotic and the poetic act are symbolic (PLF, 261). A fetishist will, in a *malign* way, treat garments of his beloved as substitutes for, or symbols of, her. It is well to remember at this point that the "normal" giving and cherishing of trinkets or locks of hair among lovers is an attenuated form of the same attitude. A poet, on the other hand, may, in a *benign* way, use "fetishistic" metaphors or symbols as elements of his poem, as, for instance, Alexander Pope does in *The Rape of the Lock*.

The differences between neurotic behavior and the poetic act are, however, just as clear. The very fact that poetry, as an articulate verbal *act*, is distinct from neurotic *compulsion* contributes to a transcendence—although a compulsive urge may, of course, underlie the *making* of a poem. Specifically, Burke notes three areas in which he would like to modify psychoanalysis before transferring its basic methods into criticism:

(1) Freud reduces every complex to its libidinous element; yet every simplification, Burke notes, is an oversimplification. And, while Freud's type of oversimplification may be perfectly efficient as a therapy "for the class of neurotics [he] encountered," Burke would replace this "essentializing" reductionism by a "proportional strategy" designed to take every unit in the complex equally into account (PLF, 261–62). (2) Freud overemphasizes the patriarchal pattern. In the light of Malinowski's anthropological researches about totemistic societies and the corresponding matriarchal patterns of neurosis and myth, Burke has adapted his version of psychoanalysis accordingly. Such a modification, he holds, becomes especially necessary in the transference of psychoanalysis to esthetics, because the basic pattern of art, as he sees it, is the rebirth ritual in which the maternal factor is predominant (PLF, 273–74). (3) In adapting psychoanalysis to literary criticism, two new elements, Burke feels, have to be introduced to make a fully rounded approach possible. Psychoanalysis concentrates on the personal unconscious, or "dream"; in art, an audience-regarding element ("prayer") and a reality-oriented element ("chart") also play an important part (PLF, esp. 267–68, 281, 284). (A fourth corrective is not explicitly stated in the "Freud" essay; but it accounts for another significant "post-Freudian" element in Burke's theory: in addition to an analysis of a work's image complexes in

isolation, Burke places major emphasis on the positional element, or the progression of images. But there is a more appropriate context for discussing this point later on.)

(b) *Dream, prayer, chart.* These three terms, then, are the trigonometrical points of the theory of literature codified in *The Philosophy of Literary Form.* They can perhaps be made less forbidding by substituting a set of corresponding terms: they are the imaginative (or expressive), the communicative (or affective), and the descriptive (or mimetic) aspects of a work. In the subsequent *Motivorum* project, the corresponding terms are *Symbolic, Rhetoric,* and *Grammar.* Yet since the *Grammar* explicitly deals with the purely internal relationships of a symbol system, it is advisable to look for ways in which "chart" itself contains elements that point away from the strictly mimetic to the intrinsic.

These three subdivisions of a work are in no way antithetical or mutually exclusive. On the contrary, they are characterized by a convenient convertability, with dream as the central aspect. This transmutability explains, for instance, the ease with which they cooperate in Burke's basic definition of a poem. As *chart,* it "sizes up" or names a situation, just as a proverb does; as *dream,* it does this naming in a "strategic" or stylized way, "magically" expressing the speaker's attitude; and as *prayer,* it conveys this attitude by means of the public content of language. Hence the definition: Poetry is the "adopting of various strategies for the encompassing of situations. These strategies size up the situations, name their structure and outstanding ingredients, and name them in a way that contains an attitude towards them" (PLF, 1).

Such namings are symbolizations in Burke's sense of the word. They face three ways: toward the situation, which they size up; toward the intrinsic structure of the work, which they constitute; and toward future situations, which they help to interpret. In fact, any verbal formulation answers to this description. Burke's example of the 1930's, "planned economy" versus "regimentation," shows how single words size up the economic structure of the New Deal and do so in a way which contains and conveys factional attitudes (PLF, 4). Referring to a more recent situation, Hugh D. Duncan points out that the "name we give to poverty largely determines how we fight the war against it": Are the poor "lazy, degenerate . . . cunning, ignorant . . . victimized, or unfortunate?" [5]

It may be noticed that in the above definition of poetry an explicit reference to the communicative dimension is missing. Is it taken for granted, or is this omission in any way significant? As defined, *prayer* sums up the "communicative functions of the poem, involving the many considerations of form, since the poet's inducements can lead us to participate in his poem only in so far as his work has a public, or communicative, structure" (PLF, 6); "in short, all that falls within the sphere of incantation, imprecation, exhortation, inducement, weaving and releasing of spells; matters of style and form, of meter and rhythm, as contributing to these results, and thence to the conventions and social values that the poet draws upon . . ." (PLF, 282). The magic and the poetic realms are fused.

"Style" and "form"—such terms call back the dialectic esthetic of *Counter-Statement,* where form, though rooted in the original symbol, was attributed an *independent generative power.* But in *The Philosophy of Literary Form,* Burke regards its *origin* in the symbolic dimension as essential, not its antithetical efficacy. In the Freud essay, "prayer" had been introduced explicitly as a corrective to the psychoanalytic "dream" monism, but two years later the key passage on the relationship of "prayer" and "dream" reads: "I am merely suggesting that, when you begin to consider the situations behind the tactics of expression, you will find tactics that organize a work technically *because* they organize it emotionally. The two aspects, we might say Spinozistically, are but modes of the same substance" (PLF, 92). As Burke notes later in reference to Spinoza, the substantive equation of God with nature (*Deus sive natura*) prepares for the elimination of one of the two substances (PC, 188n; GM, 72). By this argument, the statement about the identity of the technical and the emotional organization of a work prepares for the eradication of either emotional or technical form. In this case, emotional form, the "symbolic," becomes the *cause* of technical organization.

A similar reduction may be noticed when the term "chart" is subjected to a microscopic scrutiny. It is originally defined as the "realistic sizing up of situations" (PLF, 6) and, as such, is primarily associated with the proverb. A proverb also sizes up a situation —in fact, it encompasses many: it names "typical, recurrent situations" (PLF, 295). Thus, "Whether the pitcher strikes the stone, or the stone the pitcher, it's bad for the pitcher" is suited to characterize any number of situations in which an individual or a small group opposes a powerful authority. As Burke notes, "these situations are all distinct in their particularities . . . ; yet all are classifiable together under the generalizing head of the same proverb" (PLF, 3).

In applying this principle to literature, Burke identifies the adoration of the Dynamo in Eugene O'Neill's play of the same name as essentially satanic, as an "obeisance to the Catholic Devil, thus materialistically refurbished" (PLF, 42–43). The fact that Burke overrides significant differences of detail shows that "chart" is explicitly designed as a *generic* term, not as one which refers to concrete realistic details: "No matter how concrete and realistic the details of a book, they may be found, when taken in the lump, to 'symbolize' osme over-all quality of experience, as growth, decay, drought, fixity, ice, desiccation, stability, etc." (PLF, 36; cf. also 301). This quotation explicitly ties "chart" in with the *symbolic.* And there are other considerations which show how "chart" is deflected from the strictly mimetic: one and the same situation, Burke says, may be sized up by two apparently opposite proverbs: "Repentance comes too late" and "Never too late to mend" (PLF, 297). The difference lies in the fact that both contain and convey opposite attitudes: the first proverb is vindictive; the second, encouraging; and, insofar as attitude, or strategy, is involved in the naming, there is magic and the symbolic, too. Chart becomes charm. A striking instance of such a magical misnomer is the very title, *The Philosophy of Literary Form;* for "Psychology of Symbolic Action" would have been much more "realistic." Moreover, despite some basic differences, the title also echoes I. A. Richards' *Philosophy of Rhetoric* (1936), a book in many ways parallel.

(c) *Situation and strategy.* These examples show how "dream" virtually absorbs the other two components, "prayer" and "chart." They assert themselves only in such essays as "The Rhetoric of Hitler's 'Battle'" and "Antony in Behalf of the Play," two extremely perceptive but, from the point of view of literary theory, peripheral pieces. At the center of the theory, the communicative and the mimetic aspects are manifest only in reductive and twisted forms, as can be traced in the terms "situation" and "strategy." For there is a sense in which these two terms merge in Burke's theory. This observation may come as a surprise, especially if one remembers the definition of poetry as the strategic sizing-up of a situation, where these two terms are evidently differentiated from each other. But it has already been noted that "situation," as Burke uses the term, refers to concrete details only summarily and at a "high level of abstraction" (PLF, 301); and a typical, recurrent situation, or the general behind the particular, can be recognized only by verbalization—by the process of naming, which, according to Burke, is necessarily strategic. It is therefore only an apparent contradiction if Burke, in commending the poetic theory of *The Philosophy of Literary Form* as *sociological* criticism, refers to this approach variously as "grouping by situation" and "classification with reference to *strategies*" (PLF, 302, 303). In an essay first published in 1941, this equation is explicitly made (GM, 511). But it must be conceded that, at this point, criticism ceases to be sociological and becomes latently or patently psychological. This claim can be substantiated by scrutinizing the term "strategy."

In defending his choice of the term "strategy," Burke says: "Surely, the most alembicated and sophisticated work of art, arising in complex situations, could be considered as designed to organize and command the army of one's thoughts and images, and so to organize them that one 'imposes upon the enemy the time and place and condition for fighting preferred by oneself'" (PLF, 298). Yet Andor Gomme correctly asks in his recent discussion of Burke's criticism: In art, who is the enemy? [6] To the extent that the reader may be implicated, the term "strategy" as applied to art certainly is erroneous. The concern of art is not to outmaneuver the reader. But at times Burke clearly holds that art does exactly that. Thus, in his essay "Antony in Behalf of the Play," Burke analyzes Antony's speech in *Julius Caesar,* Act III, Scene ii. ("Friends, Romans, Countrymen . . ."), which brings about the reversal of that play, as a ritual for the swaying of both the Roman play-mob and the audience. A very similar ritual is at work in Hitler's *Mein Kampf,* as can be seen by comparing Burke's essay on this book with the one on *Julius Caesar.* One can note striking parallels: Hitler's insistence on the importance of a geographic center for every "movement"—a Rome, Mecca, or Munich—corresponds to the incident in the play when Antony steps down from the rostrum to gather the mob around himself and Caesar's body for the final call to action. Any movement must have its scapegoat or devil: just as Hitler found his, Brutus ironically tags this label on the "honorable men." And, just as the Nazis revealed their true face for everyone to see when they staged the pogroms of the notorious *Kristallnacht* in 1938, the Roman mob had its own little "crystal night" when, in the scene after Antony's speech, its members set about mauling Cinna, the poet, despite his protests that he is not Cinna, the assassin—an example of vicious, irrational identification.

According to Burke's principle of classification by strategies, would he not have to put *Mein Kampf* and "Friends, Romans, Countrymen . . ." into the same category? His exegeses are ingenious yet contain one flaw: in discussing the play, Burke does not adequately account for the occasions in which Antony interrupts his oration on the pretense of excessive grief and stops to listen for the mob reactions. In these instances of dramatic irony, Shakespeare strategically takes the side of the audience by assuming a perspective for the appropriate judging of Antony's maneuvers. In this sense, Gomme is correct when he observes that Burke fails to distinguish between propaganda and art.[7]

But there is another sense, overlooked by Gomme, in which Burke uses the term "strategy." In the immediate context of his definition of it, he refers to the "campaign of living." Life, then, is the enemy? Indeed, this view is immediately connected with the idea expressed in *Counter-Statement,* according to which the poet stakes out the realm of art against life. In *The Philosophy of Literary Form,* Burke distinguishes two basic strategies toward the threat of life: the attitude of pious awe (life seen as sublime) and that of impious rebellion (life seen as ridiculous). Threat is the basis of beauty (PLF, 61). In terms of symbolic action, art is viewed as an autocathartic adjustment to life, and readers who find themselves in the same situation as the poet take his work as stylistic medicine, just as the "hysteric" did in *Counter-Statement.*

Thus, all of Burke's terms, such as "prayer," "chart," "situation" and "strategy," relate back to the "symbolic." This reflexive and ultimately author-psychological nature of the theory of symbolic action becomes explicit in the *Motivorum Corpus.* There, the dimension of "symbolic" subsumes all "modes of expressions and appeal in the fine arts [together] with purely psychological and psychoanalytical matters" (GM, xix). In the fourth volume of his project on motives, however, Burke tries to transcend this psychological perspective by claiming that ostensibly "psychological" categories are implied in the very language system of man (cf. below, Chapter 9, Section V).

Nevertheless, it is clear that the central, though not altogether exclusive concern of *The Philosophy of Literary Form* is the development of a theory and of an analytical methodology of the imaginative strand in any literary work—the devising of rules for discovering the author's attitudes as disguised, and revealed, in his verbalizations. Such a method of analysis of course works best in texts in which the author's engrossment is upmost, texts that are written with earnestness and simplicity (PLF, 69–70). Also, the approach necessarily postulates a pragmatic continuity between works traditionally labeled "art" and any other type of verbal expression, practical, philosophical, scientific, or otherwise.

Indeed, Burke recommends his method for "break[ing] down the barriers erected around literature as a specialized pursuit" (PLF, 303); and, quite consistently, he always draws upon biographical material, lectures, and letters when he analyzes individual works. He does so not only to support, but sometimes even to discover his symbolic interpretations. "Use all that is there to use," is his undeniably sound critical principle (PLF, 23). The acme of critical taste is required to avoid the possible misuse of such a syncretistic principle. Burke is, as a rule, discriminating enough. He commands many skillful means of building in safety devices against a psychoanalytical oversimplification (but he is now much more lenient in his attitude toward it than he was in his Freud essay).[8] He does not normally reduce the complexities of a poem to a single cause, as psychoanalytical critics usually do.

Thus, in his remarks about Coleridge's *The Rime of the Ancient Mariner* (his main illustrative text in *The Philosophy of Literary Form*), Burke recognizes five sets of problems—esthetic, marital, political, drug, and metaphysical—as contributory to Coleridge's expressive act in the poem (PLF, 93–99). This diagnosis is not basically changed by the fact that Burke treats the drug problem as the basic burden "interwoven with [Coleridge's] many other concerns," for Burke is able to substantiate this simplification by references to Coleridge's poems and letters (PLF, 22–23, 96–99). Also, he correctly points out that none of this background information need be known in order to appreciate the poem, although he insists that such knowledge is very useful for the understanding of the "psychology of the poetic act" (PLF, 73). His position is this: "If we try to discover what the poem is doing for the poet, we may discover a set of generalizations as to what poems do for everybody. With these in mind, we have cues for analyzing the sort of *eventfulness* that the poem contains. And in analyzing this eventfulness, we shall make basic discoveries about the *structure* of the work itself" (PLF, 73).

This functional approach to a poem's structure is distinguished from other modern concepts of artistic structure by the fact that Burke places a comparatively greater emphasis on the *dynamic* aspect ("eventfulness") of a work than do most other contemporary critics, especially when they think of structure as "architectonic," as does Herbert Read,[9] or approach the problem, as T. S. Eliot does, in terms of pattern or configuration. René Wellek and Austin Warren recognize a teleological element in "structure" ("both content and form as they are organized *for aesthetic purposes*"), but they do not go substantially beyond this assertion, as far as the *dynamics* of a work are concerned.[10] In Cleanth Brooks's theoretical definition of structure ("the principle of unity which informs [the poem] seems to be one of balancing and harmonizing connotations, attitudes, and meanings"), the static idea of a suspended equilibrium predominates, though his practical criticism is much more dramatistic.[11] John Crowe Ransom's concept of structure has no immediate relevance because it does not refer to the work as a whole but serves as one of the two elements of his dialectical esthetic: namely, the basic rational argument.[12]

But then, Burke's concept of a dynamic structure is also partial, though in a different sense: it refers almost exclusively to the imaginative strand of a work, analyzable primarily in terms of the poem's imagery. At least, symbolic analysis, as Burke develops it, deals only with the "*fundamentals* of structure"; but it has the advantage that it "approaches the work as the *functioning* of a structure." And functional statements about a work are certainly more relevant than descriptive ones, just as a running commentary on a football game makes more sense when it takes tactics and strategies into account than when it ignores the game's purposes (PLF, 74). The great difficulty with this example is that the rules and aims governing and determining a football match are codified outside, and apart from, the individual game, and are binding. This is not so in literature. Therefore, in order to make his functional analysis meaningful, Burke must next lay down the rules of the symbolic game of poetry. But by the nature of their subject, they cannot be binding; they must remain suggestive.

(d) *The ritual unburdening as scapegoat symbolism.* Burke's first assumption about the symbolic act is that "the poet will naturally tend to write about that which most deeply engrosses him—and nothing more deeply engrosses a man than his *burdens*, including those of his physical nature, such as disease" (PLF, 17). Again, this statement must not be misunderstood as a straightforward endorsement of Freudianism; for Burke immediately modifies it by observing that "the true locus of assertion is not in the *disease*, but in the *structural powers* by which the poet encompasses it" (PLF, 17).

Nor is Burke the only modern writer who regards an oppression as the incentive to expression. The German poet and critic, Gottfried Benn, defines lyric poetry as the interaction between a pressing "inarticulate creative germ" in the mind of the poet and the total resources of language, as far as the poet has mastery over them.[13] And T. S. Eliot, in going beyond Benn, describes the poet in the state of writing "poetry of the first voice": "He is oppressed by a burden which he must bring to birth in order to obtain relief. Or, to change the figure of speech, he is haunted by a demon, a demon against which he feels powerless, because in its first manifestation it has no face, no name, nothing; and the words, the poem he makes, are a kind of form of exorcism of this demon." [14]

Insofar as Eliot conceives of the "three voices" not as mutually exclusive genres but as aspects of all poetry (OPP, 99), this passage has an even greater "Burkean" relevance than its intrinsic meaning might lead one to assume, although, of course, Eliot has never gone far toward the subtle systematization of this aspect which Burke achieved.

(i) *The nature of the burden.* When Burke says that a poet as a rule writes about what most deeply engrosses him, he does not refer to the overt topic or subject matter of the work. From his point of view it would, for instance, be largely irrelevant that in *The Jungle* Upton Sinclair is genuinely concerned about the mismanagement of the Chicago meat-packing industry at the turn of the century: Burke would look for the "typical situation" and for the strategy or attitude with which the author approaches his subject. To use the distinction adumbrated by John Dewey in *Art and*

Experience, that, if there is a conflict, a tension between the individual and his environment, if there is something which he "does not like," the science-minded person attempts an improvement by trying to alter the circumstances; and he might, like Sinclair, succeed. On the other hand, the poet in Burke's sense feels the discrepancy as a personal insufficiency or malaise—in short, as a burden which he will try to cope with by psychic adjustment, by a symbolic solution (PLF, 312), the "dancing of an attitude" (PLF, 9). This view is in a sense the Freudian as against the Marxist solution, though these two basic strategies are, of course, not restricted to members of these two factions. And, as has been shown, Burke's critical "Freudianism" is substantially modified.

The exact nature of this psychic oppression can best be revealed by an analysis of the work's images. In Burke's theory, this burden is inextricably bound up with the problem of identity which, as he sees it, involves a rebirth ritual—especially in an era of transition (PLF, 273). In terms of imagery, the problem of finding an identity, of forming a role, takes place at the abstract or forensic level.[15] The imagery of this level has to do with the *insignia* in poetic action which indicate the poet's way of forming his role or identity by "enrolling himself in a band" (PLF, 37)—by a stylistic declaration of what stand he takes with regard to the symbols of authority. Characteristically, Burke calls this element the *Bundschuh* ingredient of art, referring to the laced boot which the insurgents of the German peasants' uprising at the turn of the sixteenth century used as their emblem. The pun implicit in the German word explains this exotic term: *Bund* refers both to the lacing or tying of boots and the ties by which a community is bound. Such an element, Burke feels, is sometimes implicit, as in Alexander Pope's stylistic correctness with which he cast his literary vote for the "new propertied class eager for 'correctness'" (PLF, 37). More often, perhaps, it is explicit, as in the many fictional works in which propaganda merges with art. Such different works as John Bunyan's *Pilgrim's Progress,* G. B. Shaw's *Major Barbara,* and Bert Brecht's *Herr Puntila and sein Knecht* belong to this type.

"The *formation* of role, however, involves, in its working out, a *transformation* of role," because, even if one should want to become most thoroughly oneself, one would have to abandon irrelevant ingredients (PLF, 38). In this process of reidentification, one would have to leave behind one's former allegiance or enrollment; one would have to repudiate one's former life, even one's whole past lineage. Conversion involves sacrifice, killing; appropriate symbols are suicide, parricide, or prolicide. Conceivably, feelings of guilt are inextricably fused with an engrossment of this kind (PLF, 92).

Burke does not elucidate his idea of symbolic suicide, but it seems that it is one of the ingredients in Hamlet's act of jumping into Ophelia's grave, although non-symbolic psychological motivations also play a part (*Hamlet,* V.i.). At any rate, Hamlet calls out his name, "This is I/Hamlet the Dane"; and by this rash act and the assertion of his identity in terms of his valiant ancestry, and especially of his father, "who smote the sledded Pollacks on the ice," and whose name he bears, he reveals his change from an irresolute weigher of evidence to a determined avenger—a transformation which he had undergone during his journey across the sea. It may be objected that this determination has already been reached in Act IV, Scene iv, 65–66: "O, from this time forth/My thoughts be bloody or be nothing worth." But the "How all occasions do inform against me" monologue, which culminates in this resolution, is omitted from the text of 1603 and from the Folio which was prepared by Shakespeare's fellow actors Heminge and Condell. Also, Richard Flatter has cogently argued that this monologue is out of place.[16] Moreover, the rebirth theme is also pointed up in the puzzling message to the King, in which Hamlet announces his return, writing: "You shall know I am set naked on your kingdom" (IV.vii.43). "Naked" in Shakespeare's English may mean "destitute," "unequipped," or "unarmed," as in *Othello* (V.ii.261); but its more general meaning, as in Macbeth's "naked, new-born babe" (I.vii.21), might be taken to indicate that there is a pun on "naked" in Hamlet's note which reinforces the rebirth theme.

Symbolic parricide plays a part in the felling of the tree in Burke's early story, "In Quest of Olympus"; and there it was also accompanied by a transcendental change in lineage and name, from the bondsman Treep to Arjk, the thunder-god. For evident reasons, the Expressionist period of anti-authoritarian revolt was especially characterized by parricidal motives, as in Walter Hasenclever's play *Der Sohn* (*The Son,* 1914) and Arnold Bronnen's *Vatermord* (*Parricide,* 1925). A parallel phenomenon in religious life is the conversion of Saul, which involved his falling to the ground—also a symbolic dying—three days of blindness, anguish, and prayer, and his final renaming as Paul (Acts 9, 3–19; 13, 9).

Guilt, sacrifice, symbolic killing, and rebirth, are, then, the ingredients of religious conversion and of poetic ritual as analyzed by Burke. Both are ritual dramas, or scapegoat patterns. They dramatize, radicalize, or hypochondriacally exaggerate patterns of mental development which are normally experienced in an attenuated form. They differ from each other insofar as the religious sacrifice emphasizes the benign result of the killing—whether symbolic, as in conversion, or real, as in martyrdom or the Crucifixion. Imaginative literature, on the other hand, more often than not focuses on suffering and killing, with salvation or purification ambiguously implied, as for instance in much of the fiction of Ernest Hemingway and in parts of William Faulkner's work, notably in *Light in August.* In the sense that symbolic unburdening involves the kill as well as purgation, poetry is essentially tragic.

(ii) *The scapegoat.* The central figure in this reidentification ritual is the scapegoat, the vessel (man or beast) upon which primitive purification ceremonies had magically loaded a tribe's sins, whereupon it was either killed or expelled into the wilderness to perish together with its burden.[17] As Burke sees it, the poet, in writing, also transfers a burden upon a character or symbol in his work by a process which he calls the "socialization of a loss," whereby "something, deeply within, devoutly a part of one's own self," is ambiguously shared with the general public (PLF, 45).

In the poetic strategy, the sacrificial vessel need not become a scapegoat in the malign sense of the word, as in black-and-white pamphleteering. For, insofar as the scapegoat actually bears the writer's burden, he becomes by the same token a part of the writer, a benign or charismatic entity. In this sense, the "ritualistic scapegoat is felt both *to have* and *not to have* the character delegated to it," in contradistinction to the pseudo-scientific scapegoat who is an explicit projection of the purely malign intention (PLF, 45–46). To this extent, the scapegoat is also a synecdochic figure, one which is a part of the poet. Hence the attitude of ambivalence toward it, already called forth by its mixed malignity and benignity, is intensified. It suggests the necessity of *discount,* of the realization that the poetic scapegoat does not "possess intrinsically the qualities we assign to it" (PLF, 46).

This complexity and ambivalence is an additional reason for assuming that the burden expressed in the symbolic act is at the same time dissimulated and can be grasped only by enlisting cryptological methods, including image analysis. What, then, is Burke's methodology for tracking down the hidden offense, for getting at the fundamentals of poetic structure?

IV *The Methodology of Symbolic Exegesis*

Burke has frequently shown his awareness of the fact that his critical method vows him to interpretation (PLF, 69) or exegesis (ATH, 194), a continual talking off the subject (ATH, 191). To explain a poem as an unburdening is to explain a complexity in terms of a simplicity, something in terms of what it is not. Such an explanation is again a perspective by incongruity, and Burke has frequently been censured for this procedure. One of the most outspoken critics of this kind is Marius Bewley who feels that Burke's contribution to literary criticism is the formulation of a vocabulary that "insulates its user against the shock of the work of art itself" and that provides disciples with a machine to "speed away from any very exacting evaluation of a work of art." [18]

Bewley grapples with the central paradox of literary criticism without noticing it: any critic must, in talking about a poem, necessarily talk about something else at the same time. Thus, for instance, William Empson—surely a textual critic if there ever was one—explains poems in terms of what they are not, namely the dictionary.[19] Eliot's early warning of any kind of interpretative criticism is much to the point. He solves the paradox with a sword by restricting criticism to fact-finding, to "putting the reader in possession of facts which he would otherwise have missed." [20] As he himself notes, Eliot here moves in deep water; for what is "a fact"? Burke certainly provides the reader with much that he would not otherwise have noticed.

Eliot's approach to criticism dodges the hermeneutic problem by isolating interpretation as an act of experience concomitant with each individual reading of the poem.[21] But it does not follow that one must not communicate one's personal act of interpretation. In so doing, one must, however, keep in mind that one is both talking on and off the subject at the same time. Burke is fully aware of this hermeneutic paradox; Bewley, in turn, shortsightedly castigates him for a *sine qua non* of any kind of literary criticism that does not resign itself to giving factual information alone; and, by providing facts *about* a work, one does not at all discuss the work *itself*.

Burke's practical criticism starts with the completely neutral and naïve observation that "the work of every writer contains a set of implicit equations. He uses 'associational clusters.' And you may, by examining his work, find 'what goes with what' in these clusters—what kinds of acts and images and personalities and situations go with his notions of heroism, villainy, consolation, despair, etc." (PLF, 20). Even the most conscious and deliberate of poets cannot be completely aware of all these interrelationships while he is writing because the total structure of motivations, of the interrelationships of events and values becomes evident only after the completion of the work (PLF, 20).

Under these circumstances it is possible to reveal a work's motivational structure by "scissor work," by objective quotation and collation of its outstanding ingredients; and Burke's elaborate theory of unburdening provides the cues for placing the emphases in this analysis. As he sees it, there are three things to look for: (a) the dramatic alignment, what versus what; (b) the cluster of associations, or "chords," what equals what; and (c) the progression, or "arpeggio," what leads to what.

(a) *The dramatic alignment.* Since the ritual of unburdening presupposes a hidden offense, it also necessarily implies a conflict. Such a conflict can, of course, best be noted in a drama or novella where it is featured. Thus, in Clifford Odets' *Golden Boy*, the symbols around which the conflict is built are the violin and the prizefight (PLF, 69, 33–35). But tension, frequently in subtilized form, characterizes also most other kinds of writing.[22] John Keats's "Ode on a Grecian Urn" is a medium for the transcending of the conflict between beauty and truth (1943; GM, 447–63). The symbolic action in Hitler's *Mein Kampf* evolves from an opposition between the "discordant principle of parliament" and the "Ein Volk, ein Reich, ein Führer" slogan—"one people, one nation, one leader" (PLF, 69, 199–202). Of course, the opposing principles, symbols, or characters do not stand isolated but are each surrounded by a cluster of associations or adjuncts which both serve to round them out and help to mediate between them. These considerations lead to the problem of "equations."

(b) *Equations or associational clusters.* The tracing of associational clusters in a work is important because the overtones of a word are revealed "by the company it keeps." This method is derived directly from the psychoanalytical method of free associationism. Of course, the associations in a literary work are not completely free because formal, mimetic, and other considerations also play a part in determining the choice of words; but a symbolic element is certainly involved, and it can be studied. By way of an example, in turning this kind of analysis upon *The Philosophy of Literary Form* itself, the following observations suggest themselves: the logic of Burke's delineation of the scapegoat ritual proceeds by the following main steps: *unburdening* requires a *scapegoat,* which involves *sacrifice* and *kill,* which presupposes *criminality* and involves a *hidden offense;* it is hidden because it is *unutterable.* As such, it is *ambiguous;* for there are two kinds of the unutterable, the unutterably *good* (the Tetragrammaton as circumlocution for the ineffable name of the Old Testamental God, for instance) and the unutterably *bad* ("Old Nick" for Satan). Both meanings are implicit in Latin *sacer,* which is therefore best translated as *"untouchable."* Any *power* is untouchable, as for instance *electricity*—and this consideration leads Burke to make a somewhat irrelevant, hence revealing, gloss on John Dewey's and Bertrand Russell's contrary assessments of *technology* (PLF, 45–55).

This sketch delineates the formation of one cluster in *The Philosophy of Literary Form.* Since Burke insists that the individual components share in each other as the common essence of the cluster, the "hunch," as he would put it, suggests itself that, for him, technology is a burden. In perfectly Burkean manner, it would be necessary to verify this first approximation by other evidence from the same text or from other material. Thus, industrial progress, which is certainly one aspect of technology, is a dubious affair for Burke since he is concerned about the exploitation and depletion of natural resources without which progressive consumption is impossible (PLF, 6–7). Elsewhere, he has written about "Waste—the Future of Prosperity." [23] Continuing to build in this way, it would be possible to round out a given cluster in

Burke's thought, as it affects the logic of the central argument in *The Philosophy of Literary Form.* For though the logic of the argument determines the selection of details, it is no less true that the stock of details (associations of ideas in Burke's mind) determines the argument.

This demonstration of Burke's methods in action has naturally been simplified for the sake of manageability in this context, for it has concentrated on only two members of the cluster, burden and technology. Ideally, Burke requires that any reductionism of this kind be avoided and that each member be treated as equally important. Each member of the cluster synecdochically shares in the common essence. Synecdoche—a rhetorical figure by which the plural may replace the singular, the whole the part, *genus* the species, consequence the cause, container the thing contained, and *vice versa*—Burke considers to be the basic process of representation (PLF, 77).[24] Burke allots it such a central position because all these relationships can be explored and utilized when one works out a cluster of equations.

The danger of such an all-inclusive principle is that it easily lends itself to overstretching, for it might be possible to construe a synecdochic relationship between "something that occurs in the neighborhood of something else that elsewhere occurs in the general neighborhood of the symbol," as Hans P. Guth facetiously put it.[25] While synecdochic associationism may thus theoretically become too much of a good thing, in practice a critic's discrimination can stem the tide.

Two other dangers implied in the method of cluster analysis are more fundamental and thus less reparable: the first problem has to do with what Burke calls "pontification." By "trailing down equations" from poem to poem and from the poem under analysis to non-poetic texts by the same author, he tries to discover objective imaginative bridges that help him to round out a cluster. This procedure involves three related possible dangers: (1) It might lead to the slighting of the local texture in the given poem by dragging in overtones of meaning which a word may—and actually does—have in different contexts but which may in fact be ruled out by the context in the poem under inspection. (2) Certainly there are many poets who construct their poetic world as it were by a dictionary of idiosyncratic symbols. Blake, Yeats, Ezra Pound come easily to mind. But even in tracing these relationships between symbols, care must be taken not to dissolve a poem's structural unity into divergent strands of imagery webbing over other texts. (3) Finally, a long experience with this kind of analysis may result in the partly unconscious compiling of a "dream book" of poetic symbols which then could incapacitate the critic's discrimination in approaching new poems afresh, so that any tree in any poem might finally find itself regarded as a father symbol, and no questions would be asked. To be sure, Burke warns repeatedly against this danger in his later books (esp. LSA, 393; also, TO, 148).

The second difficulty concerns the fundamental term of cluster analysis, *equation.* Unless Burke uses it strictly metaphorically, the very concept of equation introduced into literary criticism as a universal principle vows him to the kind of reductionism which he would programmatically avoid; for two different images brought into poetic conjunction almost necessarily contain disparate elements of meaning over and above the common area of overlap. In a sense, it is even true that a literary work "unites the like with the unlike." [26] The matter is different when such an equation is explicitly made in the poem. But otherwise, to put it bluntly, an apple equates a pear only as *fruit,* which is already an abstraction. Also, the assertion that two poetic images are *equated* destroys the concept of an intrinsic poetic structure; for it implies that these two images are fully interchangeable, "which is to say that the equating of two terms prepares the way for eliminating one of them." Burke makes exactly this point less than two years after *The Philosophy of Literary Form.* [27]

Since, on the other hand, he insists that poetic meaning does *not* operate by mutual cancellation—that no voice in a poem is ever eliminated[28]—the only fair possibility is to conclude that he does use "equation" in a metaphorical sense, and that the substitution of a more appropriate literal term would improve his strategy in its own terms. But, before this can be done, both equation and pontification in Burke's practice must be illustrated to indicate both the method and its inherent risks. There is no intention to argue against the core of Burke's approach which is both solid and valuable; but it seems necessary right in the outset to curb some of the more extreme assertions which Burke himself later modified (LSA, 368–69; 1967 Preface to PLF). The present argument is designed to this limited end only.

In his discussion of Coleridge's *The Rime of the Ancient Mariner,* Burke rightly assumes that the explicit moral ending of the "Rime" with its preference of church over wedding must be prepared for in the poem; otherwise, it must be regarded as a structural flaw. He finds the marriage problem foreshadowed in "the murder of the Albatross as a synecdochic representative of Sarah" (PLF, 72). Yet how does the Albatross get into the same bin with Coleridge's wife? "The Albatross, we are told, came through the fog 'As if it had been a Christian soul,' . . . [and] in 'The Aeolian Harp' we are told that Sarah, the poet's wife, who biddeth the poet walk humbly with his God, is a 'Meek Daughter in the family of Christ.' Sarah and the Albatross are thus seen to be in the same equational cluster" (PLF, 71). But are they really? While the context of the *Ancient Mariner* delimits the reference to the Albatross as a Christian soul strictly to the expression of the ship's crew's purely existential joy at meeting another living creature in the Antarctic desolation, the Christianity of Sarah is connected with her homely orthodox morality, as she wants to keep the speaker from his esthetic raptures. The Albatross and Sarah thus share in *different* aspects of Christ, and the bridge is very rickety, to say the least.

This criticism of one detail, however central, of Burke's reading of Coleridge's ballad does not automatically destroy the complexity and relevance of his total interpretation; it does, however, suggest a way of improvement. Before discussing this possibility, it is necessary to round out Burke's methodology by noting his third device for charting poetic structure: progression.

(c) *Progression.* The very nature of a poem as unfolding in time causes the equation of images to shade over into progression, just as in music a simultaneous chord can be resolved into a sequential *arpeggio,* the successive striking of the notes of a chord (PLF, 75). In fact, Burke places major emphasis on the importance of the position which each symbol has in the sequence of the given poem, thereby partly redeeming the diffusive effect of a cluster analysis pure and simple. He distinguishes the "qualitative points: the 'laying of the cornerstone,' the 'watershed moment,' and the 'valedictory,' or 'funeral wreath'" (PLF, 71)—a picturesque renaming of Aristotle's quantitative parts, beginning, middle, and end. This sequential emphasis is in perfect keeping with his concept of symbolic action as a rebirth or *transformation* ritual, and it constitutes a significant advance over both Caroline Spurgeon's static method of image analysis and Freud's psychoanalysis. In this sense, Burke's method is not "statistical"; and, when he uses this term to explain the special meaning he affixes to "symbolic" (PLF, 18), he does his cause almost as much harm as good.

(d) *Cluster association as cumulation.* The fact that equation (repetitive form) and progression easily merge suggests the possibility that in all those cases in which two symbols are not explicitly equated in a poem, the concept of *addition* may describe poetic structure better than equation. The method, "what plus what," would also eliminate the reductive element inherent in equation. To use Burke's own illustration from music, a chord is not at all constituted by the consonance of equal notes but by the superaddition of different ones which harmonize.

But argumentation by analogy can at best suggest plausibility. How would this modified Burkean methodology look in action? A perfect test case is Gertrude Stein's early prose. The story of the servant-woman, "The Good Anna," for instance, opens with an almost definitory statement involving a paradox, a dramatic alignment: "The tradesmen of Bridgeport learned to dread the sound of 'Miss Matilda,' for with that name the good Anna always conquered." [29] Yet a dread-inspiring victory is not normally compatible with goodness. The reader's imagination is thus vexed and subtly incited; and, as the story unfolds, the implications of, and explanations for, this paradox are gradually revealed.

The narrative procedure is ingeniously adapted to this end, for the story progresses by a carefully controlled revelation of simple situations, and each situation is as a rule summed up in a cluster of descriptive and evaluative adjectives. As new situations unfold, the composition of these clusters changes gradually, and the pressure of the different contexts ever so slightly warp and ultimately redefine the individual members of these clusters. Anna is a "small spare german woman" who, watching and scolding hard, is a "good incessant german [foster] mother" to one of the younger maids in the household which she supervises. In her "stubborn faithful german soul" she neglects her own health, until finally a friend can "persuade even the good Anna to do things that were for her own good."

A conflicting principle is also involved in the story. "Badness," or "evil," characterizes all those persons who evade Anna's libidinous hold. In the story, this revelation is of course also infinitely subtilized by humor and allusion, and it is also subliminally related to "goodness." When the canvas of the story with its merging shades of pastel is unrolled to the end, it discloses a wide gamut of conflicting ingredients in the master adjective "good," corresponding to a complex and fascinating characterization of the titular person. "Good" takes on strong overtones of right, righteous, self-righteous, selfish, charitable, exploited, thrifty, domineering, clannish, "german"—and what may appear as contradictory in this bare series exists as a progressive suspended equilibrium of forces in the text.

It does not follow that any one of these adjectives is equal with "good" or any other member of the cluster, certainly not within this story. Thus, for example, if "good" were replaced in the opening sentence—". . . for with this name the [righteous (selfish, thirfty, clannish)] Anna always conquered"—the paradoxical tension, perhaps even the whole meaning would evaporate; and a title like "Anna, the Exploited Servant" would suggest a different story altogether. The symbolic action in this story—an exemplary redefinition of "goodness"—requires that every word should be irreplaceable: not even a close associate should be able to act as substitute. Cumulation and variation, not equation and substitution, are the structural principles of this text.

The symbolic analysis, modified by these considerations, would chart the imaginative strand of any literary text by considering the following points: (1) Conflict or opposition: what is the dramatic alignment? (2) Repetition: what, if any, are the equations? (3) Cumulation, or apposition: in what way do associational clusters agglutinate? Watch for dissimilarities as well as for similarities! (4) Progression: what are the transformations? At what critical points do they occur? (5) Implied in this question is: what, if anything, is left behind?—an attenuated way of looking for what, in extreme forms, is the sacrifice and the kill.

The analysis of symbolic action is designed to discover what the critic thinks the poem might have done for its author, and the author for the poem, thus discovering what it does for him (the critic) and possibly for others. Exactly twenty years after *The Philosophy of Literary Form,* Burke wrote: "It is the *critic's* job to attempt systematically specifying the principles of composition that he finds (or thinks he finds) embodied in the given poem" (TO, 194). Apart from the inevitable subjectivism to which it vows the critic, this approach also contains the equipment for overcoming the subjective stance and for approximating objectivity. For, since its methodology is openly stated, successive critics can check every interpretation. If they should find that a previous interpretation does not account for all the elements which they discover in the work under inspection, they can replace it by a more inclusive and unified one. In this cumulative process of approaching objectivity, the critical method stands the pragmatic test, while at the same time the literary work shows its worth by revealing new aspects of its structure.

CHAPTER 7

Still Points

WHILE Kenneth Burke's critical and philosophical work is characterized by, and redoubted for, its formidable dialectical prowess, his poetry excells by its immediacy and absoluteness. Like Herbert Read,[1] he defines the lyric as the expression and evocation of a "unified attitude towards some situations more or less explicitly implied" (BM, ix). In this sense, the poem sums up a motive; it is a *moment* which "summarize[s] the foregoing and seminally contain[s] the subsequent" (GM, 32). Thus, whereas as a dramatist one must immerse oneself into the relativity of the flux to show the action as it unfolds, "in one's moments, one is absolute" (BM, ix).

During his whole literary career, Burke has counterpointed his Dramatistic quest by such lyrical moments, distilled pivotal points of his experience. As early as in 1917, he contributed verse profusely to a University of Ohio undergraduate magazine, *The Sansculotte*. He continued to write and publish poetry over the years. In 1955, finally, he brought out his first volume of poems, *Book of Moments,* which contains a selection of previously published verse and of hitherto unpublished pieces. His *Collected Poems: 1915–1967* appeared in 1968.[2]

Book of Moments can profitably be read backwards; for, since its arrangement corresponds roughly to the inverted order of the poems' composition or publication, such a procedure sheds light on the author's development as a poet.

I *Juvenilia*

The first poems—"sheer juvenilia" (BM, xi)—are what first poems ought to be: exercises in how to say it about spring and longing, the moon, the pond; about death, certainly; and revolt. Among these poems is a remarkably decadent prose poem in

French, "La Baudelairienne." [3] The verse, on the whole, is the freest of free verse, with the exception of an occasional closely knit sonnet. Greek mythology frequently serves as a foil. Quite often, the tone is rhapsodic, dithyrambic; in other instances, the young poet puts on the "Armour of Jules Laforgue": [4] romantic irony, sometimes anticlimactically tagged on to the end of a poem in the traditional way of Heinrich Heine, but also, more Laforguean, incorporated into the immediate context of the high sentiment.

The following passage is a representative example of this early phase, the first stanza from "Three Seasons of Love," slightly revised from the original "The Oftener Trinity" (1917):

> When the dirty snow softens the matted grass,
> And Proserpina gathering up her garments
> Prepares to return from the dull couch of Dis,
> And the trees are busy with their fresh ornaments
> In making beautiful her path to Olympus;
> Then I love.
> I am nobly desirous—
> And as I seek my mate,
> I keep one holy eye on Heaven.
> Yet my love is that same thing
> That perpetuates the snakes.
>
> (BM, 72)

Later, when Burke moved to Columbia University, the contrast between the oppressing presence of the city and the pastoral past becomes problematic:

> No, I shall not go and look out of the window;
> A city of five million mucous excitements;
> I know of a pond now in Ohio
> Where before bed some students are sitting,
> Spring! calling us to the major cycle of conception.
> (From "*Ver Renatus Orbis Est,*" 1922, BM, 70)

II *The Music of Hesitation*

A fuller record of these mounting tensions can be found in Burke's fiction of the 1920's. But the most eloquent expression, poetically transformed, of this rift is his longer poem, "From Outside" (1929). The speaker can easily be recognized as a not so distant nephew of J. Alfred Prufrock, who also hesitated before the doors and later turned around without having spoken his mind. Yet Burke's *cunctator* is less of a social person—he does not even enter; he is more intense in his internal conflict, and addicted to the rhetoric of a subtly orchestrated, plastic blank verse. He

> Passed through the tunnelled length of corridor,
> Mounted the shaft of squarely winding stairs.
> (With each new floor ascended he could peer
> Down the dark well upon his increased absence.
> . . . .
> Slowly, he said, I rise above the street—
> Until he stood beneath the milky dawn
> Of an internal, sunless, angled sky,
> Stood there and waited, asking—should he knock.
> (BM, 62)

Judged quite apart from the meaning, the sheerly melodic beauty of the vowel cadences in the last four lines is exceptional. It is reinforced by consonant effects such as the dominant liquids and nasals which are finally contracted into a cluster, "internal, sunless, angled," where the same consonant sequence, *n-l,* is repeated with varying overtones and in a different timing: *nl, n/l, ngl.* The pattern of orchestration is further complicated by the alliteration of different combinations of *s,* predominantly the *st-* and *sk-* groups, including the internal one in "asking." The *sk-* group carries perhaps the most beautiful effect of all, the augmentation, with variation, in which this passage ends: "asking—should he knock," *sk, sh—k.*

Burke has later expertly analyzed other manifestations of this device in "On Musicality in Verse": "If a [musical] theme has been established in quarter notes, the composer may treat it by augmentation in repeating it in half notes. . . . In poetry, then, you could get the effect of augmentation by first giving two consonants in juxtaposition and then repeating them in the same order but separated by the length of a vowel" (PLF, 372). The augmentation in the line from "From Outside" is even greater than by one vowel. Thus, this section of the poem ends as though by a held organ chord at the end of a hymn, which is suddenly cut off, just preceding the shock of the crisis: "asking—should he knock."

Later on in the same poem, the reversal is achieved by means of a completely objectified epiphany in the "Metaphor of Jack in the Bandbox":

> The cover of this box is made secure
> By a small catch of wire which, when released,
> Permits the lid to open with a snap
> And lo!—spring-driven, out pops a villainous head,
> Thereat to wag and compliment and grin,
> Parading his lewd presence here among us.
> (BM, 65)

After this moment of truth, the revelation of an internal tension in sexual terms, the speaker, following Jean des Esseintes and Henry Ryecroft, withdraws to the vicarious experience of "articulate, analytic sound"—books (BM, 67).

III *Social Commitment—with a Difference*

In the next poems, which appeared in *The New Republic* and in *The New Masses* after five years of silence as a poet, Burke emerges with a new tone—witty, direct, satirical—and with a new social consciousness. In this militant poetry of ideas, the city/pond rift recurs as the industrialist/Communist controversy, as in "Buildings Should Not Be Tall" (1934):

> In such granitic utterance they [the masters] reveal
> Self-portraitures of greed that rose up, when
> A grasping brood expressed in stone and steel
> Its detestation of its fellow-men.
> (BM, 55)

"Plea of the People" (written 1933), "For a Modernist Sermon" (published 1938), and "Industrialist's Prayer" (1939) are outstanding poems of this kind. Despite the propaganda element contained in them, Burke's political allegiance was more to a "Thoreau-going party of one than the one-party state," as Gerard P. Meyer put it in a delightfully Burkean and precise way.[5]

Scanning the political development of the time, Burke also has a most acute observation about the rise of nazism ("Arose the Teutons yapping with belief"):

> It was the best they drew on for their worst—
> It was the nation's greatness that did fall—
> They were by mental benefits accursed,
> And in their madness, metaphysical.
> (From "Offerings for the Time Capsule," BM, 50)

IV *Doxologies and Flowers of Dramatism*

The end of the 1930's marks Burke's transition from overt political concerns to the rounding out of his philosophical world view, Dramatism. A poem of 1939, variously entitled "Dialectician's Hymn" or "Dialectician's Prayer," foreshadows this program. With the much later "Neo-Hippocratic Oath," it is the most compact poetic statement of Burke's purposes. Written in the form of a doxology and a prayer, it exemplifies the use of the optative as the essential mode of expression in Dramatism:

> Hail to Thee, Logos,
> Thou Vast Almighty Title,
> In whose name we conjure—
> . . . .
> May we compete with one another,
> To speak for Thy Creation with more justice—
> Coöperating in this competition
> Until our naming
> Gives voice correctly,
> And how things are,
> And how we say things are
> Are one.
>
> (BM, 39, 40)

To whom is this prayer addressed? To Burke's god-term of Dramatism, a deified rhetorical figure: "For us/Thy name a Great Synecdoche/Thy works a Grand Tautology" (BM, 41).

Whereas "Dialectician's Prayer" is a Dramatistic metaphysics, "Neo-Hippocratic Oath" uses the Hippocratic Oath of physicians as the point of departure for an ironic, yet not at all malicious, statement of Burke's comic and humane ethics. It begins: "I swear by Apollo . . . /I will do as well as method shows me how" (BM, 8). "Do as well"—the pun promises both methodic effort and foreshadows the hope of prosperity expressed in the concluding stanza. Among the commitments of those who take the real Hippocratic Oath is the support of their teachers in times of destitution, which becomes much more ambivalent in Burke's version:

> Those who taught me
> I'll make into parent substitutes—
> and if they are in need
> I'll join in raising funds for them.

The promise not to "aid a woman to procure abortion" is "spiritualized":

> To no woman will I give a deadening device
> designed to keep her from conceiving
> bright new thoughts.
> (BM, 9)

The obligation of professional assistance is similarly transformed: "I'll try to show when ills might be outwitted/by devilishly morbid ingenuity." And the vow of professional discretion appears with the Freudian twist of "universal slander":

> Wherever I go, I'll go asseverating for love of the art
> and not to the ends of malice or sheerly venereal appetite.
> And if I come upon unsavory private matters
> I'll keep them to myself
> except insofar as I noise them abroad to everyone
> as observations about everyone.
>
> If I live by these rules
> may I deservedly prosper.
> But if I break the rules
> may any good that comes to me
> come undeserved.

Again, one finds the Laforguean irony doubling up an idealistic promise, but with the additional twist that the high sentiment, thus cut to size, has all the chances to continue as a humbler, more realistic motive. "Neo-Hippocratic Oath" again shows Burke as the humane moralist that he is. The poem is characteristic of his later poetic style, which may best be described as *parlando*—certainly not colloquial, but permeated by a conversational tone.

If Burke's earliest poetry was engineering with sentiments, and the main bulk of his political and Dramatistic poetry, engineering with ideas, he is also capable of a third kind of poetry, engineering with words. Thus, whereas the two great Dramatistic poems are two spiritual focal points, other moments offer a lowlier distillate, "Alky, Me Love," or such sardonically mellow trifles as "Temporary Wellbeing." Other poems of this kind—night thoughts, frequently—are a credit to Burke's musical ear, as is the slightly Cummings-inspired "Lullaby—for Oneself as Adult Male," which begins:

> O'er soft the gentling soft you smoothly on—
> In bringing in compliance to away—
> The go, the going, ought-to-go, and gone
> Give us
> Forgive this unforgiving day.
>
> (BM, 49)

Then again, he is capable of refreshingly shameless puns, as in the reminiscing "An Old Liberal Looks to the New Year, 1953," appropriately written in doggerel, in which he complains that "the social conscience of '35/Becomes the treason of '53," for, among other things

> You said, "Let's help Democracy in Spain."
> Well, lad, I think you'd better say again.
> Such attitudes are now deemed vile and ranko,
> To be quite Franco.
>
> (BM, 18)

Pun, perspective by incongruity, and wisdom are the tools at work in Burke's "Flowerishes," where Elizabeth Batterham-Burke's graphic art contributed to the flowering of his long-standing interest in epigrams, aphorisms, and proverbs. "Beware the Ideas of March"—"We moderns are not head-hunters; but we like to collect the heads that head-hunters hunted"—"If you can learn to benefit from adverse criticism, your enemies will work for you without pay"—such gems, together with a grain of tinsel, are graphically arranged in different type, upside down, in slanting lines, back to back and around the corner, in curving comet tails, or regimented in flower beds. Not strictly a poem, each epigram is nevertheless a "moment," and the total configuration a cause of delight.

V *Mastery of the Low Voice*

"Flowerishes" and their wisdom indicate yet another style of Burke's poetry, low-voiced, wise, musically perfect, calm—with an occasional edge muted by pun or metaphor. One poem of this kind deserves full quotation:

> I knew a man who would be wonder-wise
> Having been born with both myopic eyes
> Scratched in again.
>
> "Than tyrannous moments, what more absolute,"
> He asked, "except the motionless pursuit
> Of us by pain."
>
> Note squirrel on log, how pert, now in, now out—
> But classicists find either too much drought
> Or too much rain.
>
> (Wise, eyes, again
> Absolute, pursuit, pain
> Out, drought, rain)
>
> ("Problem of Moments," BM 3)

This impeccable poem begins with a compressed and inverted nursery rhyme, and leads through an emphatically unidiomatic question, whose form yet is in perfect keeping with the structure of the English language. The poem culminates in the vivid sketch of a nature scene reminiscent of William James's representative anecdote of pragmatism[6]—an association reinforced by the appended reference to absolutist classicism. Each stanza is, as it were, summed up in a rhyme-word; and the simple repetition of all rhyme-words in their order in the end musically echoes the whole poem. Marianne Moore praises this poem as a masterpiece;

it would justify her apostrophe of Burke as a "poet in what he says and in knowing how what is said has been said," even if it were his only one.[7]

Other poems in this or a similar style include his tribute to John Crowe Ransom, "Dawn in Autumn in Vermont," where he recommends that "All shrewd wisemen/Should buy into Vermont" because in Vermont industry is receding (CP, 177). If it is the old anti-industrialist who lurks behind these lines, it is, perhaps, the pastoral poet of the pond in Ohio who says in "And Here I Am, Fighting Dandelions":

> I patrol the lawn, resenting how they spread
> like a foreign policy.
>
> At times I catch one *in flagrante delicto*
> (in fragrant delight?)
> in an orgy of miscegenation with a bee,
> without benefit of clergy.
>
> (CP, 203)

In his beautiful "Assertion to End On," he finds himself "saying thanks in principle/from amidst much bepuzzlement." He describes the feeding of chickadees during one winter ("greedy wild frail bodies/their cold clutch on our fingers"), thus earning "the rights of spring," and ends:

> Yes, by far (I guess)
> the chance to have lived
> outdoes
> the need to die.
>
> (CP, 294)

Burke's poetry at its finest pleases by the absence of pose, its directness and honesty earned by a simple verbal, musical grace, with occasional touches of what he calls the "flat-tire of satire" (BM, 94). Its attractiveness differs from the primarily intellectual brilliance which the reader of modern poetry is accustomed to find in the troubled complexity of the texts, as when almost the total range of a word's dictionary meaning is compressed into its occurrence in a poem. Thus, in Allen Tate's phrase from "Death of Little Boys," "while round his sturdy belly gleam/Suspended breaths, white spars above the wreck," "suspended" is justified in many ways: because the dead boy's breath has stopped ("to suspend payment"); because the boy is now debarred from the privilege of life ("to suspend from office"); because, as explained in the subsequent metaphor, the breath is visualized as hanging above the body; and, perhaps, because, according to popular belief, the soul escapes together with the dying breath and hovers about the corpse for some time (analogous use to "solid particles suspended in a liquid").

Occasionally, Burke aims at similar effects of compression, though not usually concentrated in a single word. Normally, he does so by a technique of altered quotation and oblique allusion similar to Eliot's practice, as in "Problem of Moments." Another quite complex literary allusion is, for instance, the telescoped reference to Eliot's *Waste Land* in "The Wrens," a poem which is otherwise more reminiscent of William Carlos Williams:

> Mark the city as a place where no
> Wrens sing, as though April were seas of sand,
> With spring not the burial of lilac,
> but heat quaking above stone.
>
> (BM, 43)

But telescoped quotation, verbal complexity, and ambiguity—with the exception of the pun—are techniques which Burke uses only occasionally. W. C. Blum (J. S. Watson) accurately sums up Burke's poetic achievement: "Although his straightforward verse is a long way from the puzzles of metaphor to which we are accustomed, I think that much of it deserves to be called poetry by virtue of fertile invention—of surprises and insights that are neither images in the ordinary sense, nor conceits, nor even jokes, but might be described as 'perspectives.' "[8] As a poet, Burke stands outside the mainstream of the so-called modern metaphysical poetry. His poetry of moments is rather related to the work of such other outstanding contemporaries as William Carlos Williams and E. E. Cummings.

A Burkean moment is of course not at all identical with Eliot's still point where "there would be no dance, and there is only the dance." It is not axle-tree nor hub. Such moments could be visualized as the ever-alternating points of a wheel's circumference which, while continually rotating, are yet at a standstill in relation to the advancing vehicle. These poems punctuate the Dramatist's quest. In the *Collected Poems,* this quest extends toward the Lord in the punning form of the "Law-Word" (CP, 290, 293), toward God in the Sanskrit form of "huta," the Petitioned (CP, 295), and ends with a prayer,

> Oh lead me
> to the dew
> at dawn
> in
> First-
> Land.
> (CP, 296)

The "First-Land" which Burke has reached in his discursive writings is the mental empire of Dramatism, the landscape, as it were, of his coherent and consistent views of how men act, react, and interact *in principle.*

CHAPTER *8*

Dramatism

BURKE'S culminative world view rises from his analysis of literary works in terms of ritual drama as described and applied in *The Philosophy of Literary Form.* All his subsequent writings are devoted to the rounding out of this position: *A Grammar of Motives* (1945), *A Rhetoric of Motives* (1950), *The Rhetoric of Religion: Studies in Logology* (1961), and *Language as Symbolic Action: Essays on Life, Literature, and Method* (1966). Within the scope of this study, it is impossible to present a detailed analysis of the 1600 closely packed argumentative pages of this *Motivorum Corpus.* What can and needs to be done is (1) to show how Dramatism grows out of *The Philosophy of Literary Form;* (2) to sketch the main themes of the four books and their interrelationship. Since in this phase of his thought, and particularly in the last two books, Burke proceeds not so much by argumentative progression as by reflectively circling around the object of inquiry, the most viable shortcut to the essence of his speculations is perhaps to tack on to the key terms and, by exploring their implications primarily in view of a Dramatistic poetic, round out a small summary cycle of terms of its own. The final objective is (3) to make some notes toward a general assessment of Dramatism as an epistemic system.

I *The Seeds of Dramatism*

If only incipiently Dramatistic, Burke's method of symbolic analysis certainly is *dramatic.* The search for an alignment of forces and for a scapegoat pattern in a literary work defines it as such. Accordingly, ritual drama is considered as the "hub" or *Urform* not only of literary works but of all acts in the social sphere (PLF, 103–06). One of the "Twelve Propositions" reads: "*Human* relations should be analyzed with respect to the leads discovered by a study of drama" (PLF, 310). In *Attitudes toward History,* Burke had presented Western history as a five-act drama. He also repeatedly identifies his dramatic approach with dialectic (PLF, xx, 109, etc.).

This dramatic approach develops into Dramatism when Burke, by reflecting upon the general principles of his method, turns it into a methodology and enlarges it into a general system of thought. In *The Philosophy of Literary Form,* the first explicit traces of Dramatism occur marginally. Its terminological backbone, the pentad, that is to say, the five terms—"act," "scene," "agent," "agency," and "purpose"—which Burke at that time finds indispensable but sufficient for locating and distinguishing motivational elements, is first mentioned in a footnote (PLF, 106n).[1] There, he also states the purpose of the *Motivorum Corpus:* to develop conceptual tools for the "imputation" of motives; later, he uses less dyslogistic synonyms such as "attribution," "postulation," and "statements about motives": "What is involved, when we say what people are doing and why they are doing it?" (GM, xvii).

This concern amounts to an expansion of the "prophecy after the event" approach which characterizes the symbolic analysis of literary works. It involves a high degree of abstraction. Imagine observing a street scene from an airplane taking off: in the end, it will almost look like the goings-on in an anthill. From such an anthropomorphically divine vantage point, it will be impossible to distinguish the concrete nature of each act down below; but this perspective enables Burke to arrive at permanent, universal observations beyond individual and historical change: "If I say, 'people must act,' I have made a universal statement about people in history—and with regard to this statement, 'human nature can't change' " (PLF, 100n). Burke tries to discount the high degree of abstraction involved in such an almost Spinozistic perspective *sub specie aeternitatis* by the Plotinistic-mystical strategy of supplementing the "Upward Way" toward the divine vantage point ("god-term") by a corresponding "Downward Way" back to the minutiae of life; as a rule, his Dramatistic analyses of individual works properly account for concrete details.

Another important clue to the nature of Dramatism may be found in "Semantic and Poetic Meaning" (1938–39; PLF, 138–67). In this essay, Burke is concerned with differentiating semantic (scientific) from poetic (attitudinal) naming, postulating a graded series between the complete poetic statement and the attitudinally incomplete scientific statement (PLF, 139). As he sees it, the poetic statement can be evaluated by filling in all the details that are implied in the "scope, range, relevancy, accuracy, applicability of the perspective, or metaphor" chosen (PLF, 145); the semanticist tries to be literally correct by leaving out the attitudinal factor of choice.

Rather than observing and assessing the game of life from the sidelines, the Dramatist seeks to achieve the participant's perspective: "The first [the semantic ideal] would try to *cut away*, to *abstract*, all emotional factors that complicate the objective clarity of meaning. The second [the poetic ideal] would try to derive its vision from the maximum *heaping up* of all these emotional factors, playing them off against one another, and seeking to make this active participation itself a major ingredient of the vision. . . . The poetic ideal envisions a vocabulary that *goes through* drama" (PLF, 148–49). Burke stresses the moralistic basis of Dramatism. Though not Existentialist, it is certainly a fully existential perspective.

II *The Key Elements of Dramatism*

Dramatism posits language as the basis of all knowledge. In other words, all human activities are derived from the assertion that man is the typically symbol-using animal (LSA, 3–9). Burke distinguishes four dimensions of language: the logical, rhetorical, poetical, and ethical. They are in no way mutually exclusive. The logical dimension "ranges from factual accuracy to the most highly generalized principles of self-consistency"; rhetoric includes simple persuasion and identification for the end of social cooperation; the poetic realm extends "from the rudimentary self-expressive outcry to the great epics, tragedies . . . the vigorous exercise of human utterance" as an end in itself; and in the ethical sphere, "language is the portrait of a personality." [2]

It is important to note that Burke's logic encompasses and fuses both the semantic and the syntactic dimensions of Charles Morris' semiotics, both referential meaning and the internal consistency of a symbol system. Furthermore, the terms "identification" and "identity" indicate an overlap between the rhetorical and the ethical dimension. Even more characteristic for Burke's critical position is the overlap between the poetical and the ethical in terms of the symbolic, or representative aspect: both an outcry and a portrait of personality fall under this heading.

Burke's *Motivorum Corpus* is subdivided accordingly. The *Grammar of Motives* elaborates the logic of the system and reviews the major philosophies in its light. The main tools are a concept of "substance" and the pentad terms, "act," "scene," "agent," "agency," and "purpose." The *Rhetoric of Motives* does not only conduct a parallel review of traditional theories of rhetoric; with its key term of "consubstantiality" ("identification"), it goes beyond the realm of the classical rhetoric of purposive persuasion to explore the at best half-conscious area of persuasions which a speaker or writer may put over on himself—the area of auto-suggestive rhetoric. Thus, Burke's "rhetoric" constantly merges upon the "Symbolic," and in an eloquent concluding passage on "pure persuasion" it transcends these speculations on the mysteries and spells of "courtship"—another, and certainly the most characteristic Burkean term for all kinds of persuasion—toward a universal definition of man as the "symbol-using animal" and leads up to the notion of an ultimate term, a "title of titles" or "god-term"—not God, but the court of last instance to which an integrating dialectic can carry speculation.

The *Rhetoric of Religion* appropriately takes up where the *Rhetoric of Motives* leaves off and rounds out the heavenly court or "cycle of terms" by means of logological analyses of biblical and theological texts. *Language as Symbolic Action,* an annotated collection of essays published over the last sixteen years, moves into the area of the poetic; most of the essays are Dramatistic analyses of individual literary works. Others deal with Burke's view of man, the origin of language, and psychoanalytical explorations. The ethical dimension of Dramatism has not yet been systematically explored.

(a) *A Grammar of Motives.* From the point of view of the Dramatistic logic, Part I, "Ways of Placement,"—the section in which the basic terms are developed—and Part III, "On Dialectic," are the most important parts of the book; Part II, "The Philosophic Schools," uses this logic to place the major philosophies.

Appropriately for a basic treatise on Dramatism, the book opens with a discussion of a drama, Ibsen's *An Enemy of the People,* and of the last scene of O'Neill's *Mourning Becomes Electra*

(GM, 3–6). Lavinia's final withdrawal from the world—a mental as well as a physical act—is scenically foreshadowed by the closing of the shutters of the mansion. Upon the cue of the closing shutters' "decisive bang," she "marches woodenly into the house, closing the door behind her." In this symbolically realistic way, O'Neill establishes a relationship between scene, act, and agent: the scene ambiguously, implicitly contains what Lavinia's act of entering the house renders explicit, her (the actor's or agent's) state of withdrawal from the world. It is with such relations, or "ratios," between act, scene, agent, agency, and purpose that the Dramatistic logic operates.

The first three of the pentad terms—"act," "scene," and "agent" —are borrowed from a previous dramatic theory of art and life, though certainly a less pervasive and rigorously systematic one: Henry James's, as found in his prefaces. The whole pentad may also be described as an expansion of the four Aristotelian causes—formal, material, efficient, and final—and Burke quotes passages from Aristotle which show that the Greek philosopher was also aware of an instrumental cause (GM, 228). Another important point of reference is the scholastic formula of discussion, *quis, quid, ubi, quibus auxiliis, cur, quo modo, quando:* "what" locates act; "where" and "when" describe scene; "who" identifies agent; "by what means" specifies agency; "why" indicates purpose, and "how" refers to attitude, the sixth term which transforms the pentad into a hexad.

According to Burke, all these considerations are necessary to locate the substance of an act. As the illustration from O'Neill's play indicates, the ratios that exist among the pentad/hexad terms are means of symbolic transformation. Characteristically, Burke defines dialectic as the "employment of the possibilities of linguistic transformation" (GM, 402); in other words, "dialectic is concerned with different levels of *grounding*" (GM, 440). Thus, by means of the act-scene ratio, environmental determinism and other materialistic philosophies dissolve the substance of an act into its material grounds or conditions; instrumentalism uses the act-agency ratio for a similar transformation, and other philosophical schools make a similar use of the other ratios.

Not repudiating these transformations which locate motivational elements outside the act, Burke postulates that the very act itself must also be a "locus of motives" (GM, 64–69). It must contain an element of arbitrariness, novelty, magic; otherwise, action would be reduced to sheer motion, and human freedom dissolved into determinism. In this connection, he quotes Coleridge to the effect that poetry—for Burke, the prototype of action—is a "dim analogue of Creation." Among the experiences which he draws upon to substantiate his claim is the writing of a long book, where the very act of writing raises intrinsic problems and purposes that were not contained in the original intention nor in any aspect of the scene, agent, or agency.

The ratios, or possiblilities of transformation, Burke says in perfectly Aristotelian-Thomist manner, have their origin in the "Paradox of Substance" (GM, 21–23). In perfectly Burkean manner, he tackles this paradox by an elaborate pun-analysis. To sum it up briefly: the concept of an act's, or a thing's, "sub-stance" refers immediately to the ground on which it stands, to its context. The nature of a thing is intrinsic and extrinsic at the same time. Scientific materialism, following Locke's epistemological empiricism, avoids this paradox by studying the extrinsic conditions only. Burke, by contrast, proposes to face this paradox squarely in its full ambiguity; for in it he discovers "a strategic moment, an alchemic moment, wherein momentous miracles of transformation can take place" (GM, 24). It involves the paradox of definition, for a thing is "de-fined" by setting it off from its contexts; hence, a thing is *defined in terms of what it is not:* Spinozistically, *omnis determinatio est negatio;* Hegelian logic also features this negative element.

Because of this paradox which the pentad/hexad terms explore, there is a sense in which they are empty, are "about nothing," just as the Kantian transcendental objects of the understanding—as against the sense-impressions—cannot be distinguished from *no objects at all.* In this sense, Burke characterizes Kant's philosophy as a philosophy about nothing and adds: "Any tyro can talk about something. But it takes a really profound thinker to say profound things about nothing" (GM, 189). With characteristic tongue-in-cheek straightforwardness, he hastens to admit that his own terms are "about nothing" in this sense.

Yet are not all a-historical systems of thought thus abstract? Burke tries to turn this liability into an asset by devising a theory of the "Temporizing of Essence" (GM, 430–40) and the corresponding method of "translat[ing] back and forth between logical and temporal vocabularies." By exploiting the pun on "first," Burke claims that logical principles (immutable cycles of terms) are frequently translated into stories about origin. In *The Rhetoric of Religion,* he treats the Book of Genesis in this way. In the *Grammar,* he offers a corresponding reading of Ibsen's *Peer Gynt* as the quest for one's self, or essence, spelled out in temporal terms. He also claims that for an *essential* description of some social structures it is irrelevant whether the factual *existence* of Freud's hypothetical "primal horde" is proved or disproved. But it is one thing to analyze literature, and another to interpret life. If Freud's psychoanalysis in terms of the primal horde is supposed to be anything but a metaphorical pastime, it must be correct in its derivations. In other words, while the conversion of historical insights into systematic superstructures (the essentializing of the temporal) can be accepted as the concomitant of some very interesting speculations, the extrapolation of a theory of history from such a system of thought leads to a dubious theory of *life;* it is, perhaps, one of the mainsprings of *myth, fiction, poetry;* and, as such, it is important enough.

Burke's choice to make "dialectical substance" the over-all category of Dramatism (GM, 56) weds him to a dialectic which does not unfold in time but leads back to imputed causes—a dialectic which is Platonic rather than Marxist-Hegelian. This choice also involves him in purely verbal maneuvers; and there is hardly a contemporary writer who is more adept than Burke at tracking down the verbal intricacies of different kinds of discourse, which are realities in their own right. To appreciate his skills as a literary critic, it is, however, not necessary wholeheartedly to embrace his fairly nominalistic assumption that "men's linguistic behavior . . . reflects real paradoxes in the nature of the world itself" (GM, 56).

(b) *A Rhetoric of Motives.* Less forbidding, perhaps, than the *Grammar* with its anatomy of Burkean speculative procedure, the argument of the *Rhetoric of Motives* is also tripartite. It begins with a discussion of the "Range of Rhetoric," proceeds with a review of "Traditional Principles of Rhetoric," and culminates in a section on "Order." Probably the most important contribution of this book is the study in terms of rhetoric of an "area of expression . . . midway between aimless utterance and speech directly purposive" (RM, xiii). Only the latter would fall under conventional rhetoric. On the other hand, Burke's concept of rhetoric aims at the study of the elements of sincerity even in an ostensive act of premeditated exploitation. In this sense, the *Rhetoric of Motives* explores much material that could equally well be treated in the "Symbolic," since it is largely concerned with author-psychological matters. These aspects are, however, treated here because they relate to the study of the "ways in which the members of a group promote social cohesion by acting rhetorically upon themselves and one another" (RM, xiv). Burke fully adopts Malinowski's idea of "phatic communication." [3]

The book's theme is introduced by a contrasting of Milton's *Samson Agonistes* and his *Areopagitica*—a tragedy and a propagandistic speech (RM, 3–5). While the purpose of the latter is obvious and direct, Burke sees the use of the former in Milton's identification with Samson and the corresponding symbolic solution of his own political problems as a Puritan under the Restoration. In keeping with the poetic of *The Philosophy of Literary Form*, the poet's identification with a suicidal situation and its imagistic-imaginative transcendence is interpreted as a ritual of rebirth, of transformation, hence as a scapegoat pattern. This pattern could be sloganized as "learning by identification and vicarious victimage."

Burke conceives of this process as the "tragic rhythm of action" (already developed in the *Grammar of Motives*). He takes his cue from the Greek proverb, "*ta pathema mathemata*," the suffered is the learned, which is strikingly echoed in the scholastic formula, *intelligere est pati*. Expanding the Greek adage, Burke develops a tripartite rhythm, *poiema*, *pathema*, and *mathema:* the original purposive *act* involves the agent in countervailing forces, which in turn bring about *suffering;* and this passion leads to a new *insight* as the basis of a new purpose or act (GM, 38–41). In this pattern it is possible to discern the emotionally keyed-up Hegelian triad, *thesis*, *antithesis*, and *synthesis*, as well as an intensification of Charles S. Peirce's pragmatistic pattern of the clarification of ideas: *belief* (rules for action) brings about *doubt*, hence thought, which in turn leads to a new *belief* expressed in action.[4]

For Burke, this tragic rhythm is the fundamental epistemological pattern (LSA, 367–68). More specifically, it serves as an excellent tool for the analysis of ritually tragical elements in imaginative literature in general. In the form of *purpose*, *passion*, and *percep-*

tion, Francis Fergusson has put it to brilliant use in his reading of tragedy.[5] Of course, this pattern also applies to the analyses of "identification" in literature in which Burke is engaged in his *Rhetoric of Motives.*

The key term, "identification," as used by Burke, covers three ranges of meaning: (1) *symbolic:* the author may identify with his fictional hero, or the speaker with the import of the thought and images of his speech; (2) *chart:* the thing or act is identified with the name or image which refers to it; and (3) *communication:* the audience may identify with the author's identifications.

"Identification," especially in its second sense, is evidently derived from the concept of "equation" (cf. above, Chapter 6, Section IV b), which also shades over into the third sense; for, insofar as an auditor "identifies" with what is spoken, he becomes "consubstantial" with its substance (and indirectly with that of the speaker). In the sense that this psychological phenomenon has a powerful political effect, "identification" is by the same token a factional, propagandistic, agitatorial term: Burke explicitly notes that the term is compensatory to "division"; he also notes that by the paradox of substance rhetorical "consubstantiality" does not override the difference of substances (RM, 21–22).

Hence, identification as here used is an analogical term (one that recognizes both identity and difference), though Burke tends toward a rhetorical overplaying of the aspect of identity. For this reason, when the term is used in the discussion of art, the aspect of *identity* must be discounted perhaps more than the literal meaning of the term "identification" can yield. For certainly a work of art captivates the mature observer only in the sense that it invites him to perceive but leaves him his freedom of decision and judgment; it elicits an attitude which can best be described paradoxically as identification = non-identification.

This dialectical quality of the esthetic experience is neatly adumbrated by the term "courtship" which Burke appropriates and explores in Part III of the *Rhetoric of Motives* in expert readings of Shakespeare's *Venus and Adonis,* Castiglione's *Il Cortegiano,* Kafka's *Das Schloss,* and other literary works. Burke, it is true, introduces this term in a limited sense to describe the "use of suasive devices for the transcending of social estrangements" (RM, 208). But since, by his adroit way of using it, he brings out the social, psychological, romantic, rhetorical, and hierarchic connotations contained in its aura, "courtship" develops into a felicitous master term for symbolic analysis and, beyond this area, characterizes that aspect of Burkean dialectic which is similar to the Socratic philosophical erotic.

Exploiting the pun on "courtship," Burke explores the social meaning that may be implied in a romantic courtship and coins still another term, "socioanagogic" exegesis, for this area of his criticism. The anagogic sense of a text is the fourth and ultimate sense of traditional scriptural exegesis, that which pertains to the mystery of heavenly glory. With Burke, the term is socialized because, as he puts it, the "veil of Maya is woven of the strands of hierarchy [primarily that of social order]—and the poet's topics glow through the mist [the mystery?]" (RM, 219).

Thus, in *Venus and Adonis,* Burke distinguishes not only the conventional erotic and the symbolic (psychological) meaning embodied in the ambivalence between woman as mother and woman as partner, but also a concealed allegorical meaning according to which the relationship between Venus, Adonis, and the boar represents the mysteries which characterize the relationship between the high, the middle, and low classes. This socioanagogic exegesis discloses, "in enigmatically roundabout form, a variant of revolutionary challenge" (RM, 217). In view of misunderstandings of this phase of Burke's criticism, it might be well to repeat that he fully recognizes and analyzes elements other than the socioanagogic one. Though any allegorical exegesis necessarily goes beyond the face-value of a text, Burke also takes the descriptive meaning into account: he is explicitly concerned with the multiple motivations in the poem under analysis. True, he always sees the motives also in terms of psychoanalysis, but in this phase of his criticism he certainly transcends any simplistic psychoanalytical reading.

If there is one basis of reduction, it may be found in Burke's ultimate rhetorical term, "pure persuasion." It "involves the saying of something, not for an extraverbal advantage to be got by the saying, but because of a satisfaction intrinsic to the saying. It summons because it likes the feel of a summons. It would be nonplused if the summons were answered. . . . It intuitively says, 'This is so,' purely and simply because this is so" (RM, 269). Pure persuasion is the archetype, the perfection or transcendence of the suasive motive. As Burke sees it, this archetype is inherent in language as a symbol system. For a language has many built-in orders of perfection. They begin at the sheerly grammatical level ("correctness") and culminate in Burke's Platonic dialectic, the hierarchic classification of all concepts up to the ultimate "title of titles," the "god-term"; pure persuasion would be one of its names.

Apart from language, man is involved in three other hierarchies: nature, which encompasses man's neuro-biological structure; society, including the division of labor; and the supernatural. The hierarchic mysteries of each offer goads for climbing or (punningly) mounting; hence they are basic to man's motivation (RM, 333). But even if all the motives springing from the natural, social, and supernatural hierarchies were illusionary, Burke feels that there is enough incentive in the "transcendent" nature of symbolism (of language in general), and man as the typical symbol-using animal would be moved by it (RM, 271). (Throughout the *Rhetoric of Motives*, the definition of man as symbol-using animal gradually emerges from "rational animal"; it differs from Cassirer's "*animal symbolicum*" by its lack of the scientistic emphasis.)

This rhetorical god-term, pure persuasion—as well as the other speculations about hierarchic mysteries—bring Burke to the border of metaphysics, or "meta-rhetoric," as he prefers to call these concerns (RM, 267). For, by the paradox of purity, which he had discussed in the *Grammar of Motives* in connection with Aristotelian metaphysics and Hegelian logic (GM, 35–38), a motive in its purity or absoluteness is identical with its opposite. For this reason absolute perfection is a transcendence. Such matters are beyond the scope of rhetoric and belong to the realm of religion. Hence, quite consistently, Burke next discusses his rhetorical way toward religion.

(c) *The Rhetoric of Religion: Studies in Logology.*[6] "Logology" is a rare word for "philology," and it has also been used occasionally for Christology in terms of John, I. In Burke, it refers to the study of the ways of words in general. Its method, "logologic" (the tracing of the logic that Burke finds inherent in words), aims at the establishment of "tautological cycles of terms" or chains of associations among words which are tracked down so persistently that they lead to a "Grand Rounding Out": the chain's first and last links interlock, and the whole cycle forms a closed complex of mutual implications. This conception is a further development of the critical method of tracking down equational image clusters in literature (RR, 182). It is based on the assumption that mechanisms of derivation, substitution, compensation, reversal, and the like, are at work not only in the psyche of man but also in his language (LSA, 407). Logology is derived from, but also transcends, psychoanalysis. One of its logical corollaries is the view that poetic invention and divine revelation are profound instances of listening to the ways of language, for "in its will is our (definition of) peace" (RR, 272).

The Rhetoric of Religion forms a trilogy of speculative pieces. It begins with an essay "On Words and The Word"; the other two are greatly involved meditations, one on St. Augustine's *Confessions,* and the other on the first three chapters of Genesis. Appropriately, the book ends with a "satyr play," an enjoyable dialogue between The Lord and His logological complement, Satan. In an eternal moment before creation, they discuss the implications contained in the divine idea of man, the "Word-User"; and they delightfully cover about the same ground through which Burke, in his own voice, gravely and cumbrously plodded in the previous parts of the book.

In an introduction, logology is analogically derived from theology. The derivation is based on the fundamental and essentially sound hypothesis that theological thought is determined by a fairly limited set of dogmas; that, therefore, a relatively narrow area, in which infinitely subtle nuances mark the difference between orthodoxy and heresy, has over the centuries been permeated most thoroughly by the scrupulous labor of acute minds for whom these matters were of prime importance; and that for these reasons theology is the one field where the resources of language *qua* language have been worked out most exhaustively. Therefore Burke thinks that he who is interested in the ways of language will find no better locus for his concerns than these documents; and, regardless of their ontological or theological truth, he can study them logologically as true documents of linguistic strategies and resources. In this way, Burke studies them purely as terminologies or as nomenclatures of persuasion: of their author's persuasions and of the exhortations of others (RR, v–vi).

To further support his concept of logology, Burke establishes six analogies between his study of words about God *qua* words (logology) and the study of God as The Word (theology): (1) As intimated above, there is a "likeness between words about words and words about The Word"; (2) "Words are to nonverbal nature as Spirit is to Matter." (3) Burke assumes, with such philosophers as Henri Bergson, that the negative is strictly a linguistic invention. One of the reasons for this hypothesis is the real rift between words and the objects they signify, in the sense that the sign is definitely *not* identical with the signified. Thus, one can cut down a tree, but not the *word* tree; or one can find rhyme words for the word tree, whereas the *thing* tree never rhymes with anything (LSA, 480). For this reason, and related ones, Burke thinks that "language theory, coming to a head in a theory of the negative, corresponds to 'negative theology.'" (4) Just as theology considers God the sum of all existence, language has an intrinsic entelechy toward classifications and classifications-atop-classifications until it arrives at the highest "god-term." (5) "'Time' is to 'eternity' as the particulars in the unfolding of a sentence are to the sentence's unitary meaning." (6) "The relation between the name and the thing named is like the relations of the persons in the Trinity" (RR, 33–34).

These analogies and assumptions are the tools of Burke's meditations on the *Confessions* and on Genesis. Although there is not the space to discuss any of them in detail, it is possible and necessary to indicate their general nature and purpose. This can be done by showing how the prime cycle of terms, that of *order,* begins to take shape. This discussion occurs in the essay on Genesis.

As Burke himself frequently points out, the logological approach amounts to a translation of a narrative into a cycle of tautologies, with the additional claim that this cycle ideally exists in an a-temporal mode prior to its unfolding in time. This idea is implied in Burke's fifth analogy, and it posits the logical priority of a timeless terministic cluster to its restatement in a temporal sequence. A logological cycle would be the eternal ground of an action, and logology the "theological" ground of Dramatism.

Thus, the beginning of the Creation narrative has the following logological form (Burke approaches the matter more indirectly by way of the concept of "covenant" in Hobbes's *Leviathan*): the opening words, "In the beginning," are a narrative translation of the concept of logical priority. The creation is an ordering of chaos. "Order," the key term, involves "disorder" as the logical ground of order and as an eternal threat consequential to order. Order also implies an "ordinator," an ordering agent. For everybody else, order is a "command," expressed in terms of a "covenant" between the ordinator and the subject—provided that the subject can use language. But for man, the "symbol-using animal," command, a negative or "thou-shalt-not," allows for both "obedience" (subjection) and "disobedience" (sovereignty, but of a "counter-orderly" nature). This is "free will," the capacity of "acting" (as against the "being moved, and moving" of pure physicality). Disobedience involves "guilt"; and, guilt, the need of "redemption," which automatically includes the idea of a "substitution." The "Grand Rounding Out" occurs in the idea of the "redeemer," who is both the ultimate sovereign and the ultimately obedient one (RR, 174–96).

In this compressed summary of the cycle of order, several links have been omitted; but the general idea and functioning of logologic should have become clear, as well as some of the problems it raises. Before proceeding to a criticism, however, a discussion of *Language as Symbolic Action* is in order.

(d) *A Dramatistic poetic* is the main but not exclusive concern of *Language as Symbolic Action*. In this context, however, the other psychoanalytical, linguistic, and semantic topics are dealt with only insofar as they have a bearing on poetic theory. This late stage of Burke's criticism is strongly characterized by his logologic. An essay not reprinted in the book serves perhaps best to clarify this principle as applied to criticism. In "Dramatic Form—And: Tracking Down Implications," [7] Burke explains that, in addition to his early categories of self-expression and communication (the symbolic and the rhetoric dimensions), he now distinguishes a third principle of literary structure—"consummation."

Consummation refers, as Burke puts it, to the tracking down of the implications of a terminology. Just like a mathematician or a theoretical physicist, a poet, on one level of his activity, may be concerned with such a terminological pursuit, *more geometrico*. In an interesting reading of Eugène Ionesco's *Les Victimes de Devoir*, Burke shows that, apart from whatever form the play may have because of the narrative progression of scenes, it possesses a different kind of unity insofar as all incidents radiate, as it were, like spokes from the "hub" of the title and restate the idea of "Victims of Duty" in different images and episodes. In the first scene, this central idea is manifest in a subdued way in the housewife's duty of darning socks. As the play unfolds, the dutiful victimization is transformed into more and more grotesque situations and achieves its perfection in the regressive paroxism of the hectic conclusion, when all the characters childishly and dutifully swallow mouthfuls of bread.

In the spirit in which Burke offers this terminological approach to a work—strictly as a supplement to modes of exploration which he had previously developed—this method is certainly most useful. It is an expanded and modified variant of "repetitive form," which received a new foundation in the concept of "cycles of terms." On the semantic level, it is supported by Burke's theory of "entitlement" (LSA, 359–79), according to which there is never a one-to-one relationship between a word and its referent. For instance, even if factually correct, the sentence "The man walks down the street" necessarily selects and abstracts traits from a much more complex situation. It leaves such details as the man's stature, the kind of walking, the type of street unaccounted for; in other words, it sums up, or serves as a title for, a continuum of non-verbal situations.

The sentence may in turn synecdochically (emphasizing one ingredient) be entitled "man-situation," "walk-situation," or "street-situation"; and this latter title, for instance, may become more significant than the others if the immediate or wider context contains a sentence like "There are trees bordering the street." Burke asserts that it is only at the higher levels of entitlement, in this case reached by the title, "street-situation," that a convenient shortcut between the summarizing word and the summarized object suggests a "state of affairs wherein the word is the sign of the thing" (LSA, 372). As Burke sees it, referential meaning is a very indirect affair; and in the sense that verbally man can approach the empirical objects only by entitlement (which, like society, is naturally hierarchic), "nature gleams secretly with a most fantastic shimmer of words and social relationships." And in this sense it is true that "things would be the signs of words" (LSA, 379).

This theory of entitlement which is an empirical counterpart of Emerson's Transcendentalist view of language, has a direct bearing on the Dramatistic poetic. As Burke explains in "Fact, Inference, and Proof in the Analysis of Literary Symbolism" (1954), an essay in which he quite frankly states the strong points as well as the sources of possible clumsiness of his critical method, he proceeds by a variant of the "principle of the concordance and by entitlement" (TO, 145). He "indexes" the occurrence, recurrence, and transformation of images, key terms, and other striking incidents in the order of their appearance (not in alphabetical order). One of the purposes of this indexing is to select, by objective quotation, subtitles that summarize the substance of a section, titles for chapters, and the ultimate title of titles of the whole work (TO, 154–60), thereby progressively distilling and cohobating the essence of a work. This critically discovered title need not coincide with the actual title, which may have been chosen not for intrinsic but circumstantial reasons, such as commercial ones.

Burke ultimately justifies the approach to literary works by way of terminological exploration and entitlement by his conviction that man is the symbol-using animal (LSA, 3),[8] and that terminological explorations in dialectics, poetry, and criticism are the highest forms of man's use of symbols, linguistic and otherwise. According to this view, man likes to employ his symbolic capacity —his "symbolicity," to use Burke's neologism—to the utmost, just as he likes physical exercise for the sheer fun of it. Burke explains this attraction of imaginative literature in "Formalist Criticism: Its Principles and Limitations," an essay which is certainly the best short introduction to the present phase of his criticism (LSA, 480–506).

On the basis of these later modifications of, and additions to, the analysis of literature as symbolic action, how does an actual symbolic exegesis of a work proceed? The point of departure is Aristotelian. Burke analyzes a work in view of the pleasure, or entertainment value appropriate to its genre (which need not be a conventional one). This point of departure does not at all bind him to a trifling treatment of art. On the contrary, since the poet "can transform . . . moral problems into sources of poetic entertainment" (LSA, 81), this very approach equips Burke to deal with the many dimensions of a work seen in view of a specific esthetic end. The difference between Aristotle and Burke in this point is that the former apparently conceives of the action which a tragedy imitates in quite general terms as men doing certain things, and that he does not psychologically correlate action and catharsis. Burke's concept of *symbolic* action, on the other hand, provides exactly such a correlation.

In a typical exegesis, Burke begins, by "prophecy after the event," to demonstrate how the work in question ought to be structured in view of its generic end, strategically expressed in specific terms. Thus, Shakespeare's *Coriolanus,* he points out, draws upon the civil unrest generated by the Enclosure Acts; and it exploits the ensuing class tension in the representation of a tragic victimage due to an excessive contempt of the Plebeians and to factional pride (LSA, 82). Djuna Barnes's *Nightwood* draws on lamentation as a source of esthetic pleasure, whereby a universal infantile situation is artistically transcended; the particular subject, a perverse triangle affair, is appropriate for this purpose but in Burke's view no more than a pretext (LSA, 241–42).

Yet this emphasis on a work's purpose does not bind Burke to the intentional fallacy which W. K. Wimsatt castigates in *The Verbal Icon* (1954). The purposiveness Burke concentrates on is strictly structural: it is the design which the critic can establish by a pragmatic *a posteriori* inspection of the *work* (LSA, 498). Thus, even though Coleridge's "Kubla Khan" genetically comes close to being a piece of visionary writing, under the perspective of poetics it must be analyzed in view of its esthetic effect, that of the marvelous (LSA, 204); and Burke does so in an expert reading.

Burke begins an exegesis by establishing a first structural principle. In "plotty" plays and novels, the prime mover is usually the hero, for example, Coriolanus in Shakespeare's play. In poetry and poetic prose, one can most often distinguish recurrent key images; thus, Burke hinges his reading of *Nightwood* on the verbs "turn" and "go down," which recur, particularly closely packed, in the crucial scene of the first meeting with the two main personages (LSA, 242–43). Sometimes the points of departure are several key terms underlying the imagery, as in Goethe's philosophical play, *Faust II* (LSA, 164).

Whichever may be the case, Burke proceeds by deriving the other factors involved in a work's structure from the function of the primary one. Thus, if in *Coriolanus* the hero is designed as the sacrificial figure who is to bring about catharsis in terms of a drama of social tension, his character must be marked by a drastically exaggerated form of Patrician pride in relation to the Plebeians. Coriolanus' role as a "gerundive, a 'to be killed,'" requires a killer; in the play, Aufidius becomes instrumental to this end (LSA, 84). The role of Coriolanus' domineering mother serves as the motivation for the reversals of the play and provides for the most acute form of dramatic irony: it is she who has trained the fatherless Coriolanus to become a proud warrior. *She* persuades him against his wishes to try to exploit his victory by standing for consul. But his previous training incapacitates him humbly to plead for the commoners' support. Instead, his disdainful behavior incites the wrath of the Tribunes who have him banished. Coriolanus defects to the enemy general, Aufidius, whom he has just vanquished, and leads his former opponent's army victoriously toward Rome. In the end, it is again his mother who is able to persuade him not to invade Rome but to conclude peace. Her renewed intercession ironically prepares for Coriolanus' downfall; for Aufidius blames him for giving away a total victory and has him assassinated as a traitor, thus completing the victimage.

The other *dramatis personae* are easily derivable. Coriolanus' wife Virgilia is the frail "pity" figure who contrasts with the domineering mother; his little son, who loves to rip apart butterflies, is a "chip off the old block." The tribunes and commoners are the necessary antagonists, and Menenius is the important mediator. The catharsis occurs because the play drastically overstates a societal rift which in Elizabethan England had been dramatized by the Enclosure Acts, but which a modern audience responds to because of different circumstances—not modern dictatorships, but the tensions implied in any hierarchy, any society (LSA, 89, 94). In this essay, Burke carries these considerations to further subtilizations, also touching upon points of diction. The above sketch may suffice to illustrate the way in which he proceeds in such a derivation of a play's structure.

The structure of a poem is best analyzable in terms of its imagery. Thus, in Coleridge's "Kubla Khan," Burke first distinguishes three phases: the beatific first part involving the "stately pleasure-dome," the antithetical and sinister second part dominated by chasmic imagery, and the third part in which the abyss motive—punningly contained in the phrase "Abyssinian maid"— is viewed under beatific, beautiful auspices: "A damsel with a dulcimer" to "Paradise." In the most complete and thorough reading of a poem which he has so far offered, Burke then pursues the associations of the images throughout Coleridge's other writings.

Drawing upon all contexts in which they occur, Burke elucidates the poem in a way different from J. L. Lowes, who in his monumental and certainly impressive and interesting *The Road to Xanadu* (1927) had described the poem in terms of its likely sources in other writers. In terms of poetics, Burke's approach by way of other contexts in the poetic work, in the letters and in other documents of the same writer is more pertinent than Lowes's. For the genetic approach tends to dissolve a poem's structure into the bits and pieces apparently collected from other writers. A similar danger is certainly implied in the contextual approach: the poem could dissolve into a general Coleridge dictionary, or "Coleridgese," as Burke puts it. But, as he handles and focuses his argument in this essay, he manages to avoid this danger.

To characterize the most recent phase of his critical theory and practice, it is possible to single out the following elements: (1) In the sense that Burke views poetry as a pleasurable activity exercised for the sheer fun of it, his poetic contains a hedonistic ingredient. Similar to Aristotle, he sees this element under the perspective of the generic purposiveness of the work of art. (2) Despite this over-all emotive orientation of his poetic, Burke recognizes that poetry can contribute to knowledge in at least two respects: (a) like Emerson, he commends poetry for its holistic perspective which cuts across and, hopefully, unifies the departmentalization and specialization of human activity; (b) "There is a sense in which poetry can contribute vitally to knowledge by being naturally itself, despite all its efforts to be artificial. In this sense, poetry's contribution to knowledge is limited only by the observer's non-poetic or extra-poetic prowess at diagnosis" (LSA, 368).

This clause is somewhat enigmatic. It might be interpreted and expanded—or, better perhaps, supplemented as follows: (c) If the basic motive of poetry, of imaginative literature in general, is to exercise symbolicity for its own sake, and therefore in the most thorough, accomplished, and correct way (LSA, 480–84), then it will yield the most thorough and pertinent insights into the linguistic potentialities of man; poetry *is* man's symbolicity at its highest. Ironically, this argument could be inverted by noting that for this very reason the type of criticism which makes these issues *explicit* might be regarded even higher than poetry, the *implicit* form of these matters. This would be an essentially Platonic solution, not incompatible with Burke's theories. For though he has not given up poetry, as Plato did when he set out on the "higher" pursuit of his metaphysical dialectic, Burke certainly envisages the "higher" realm of meta-rhetoric which, because of the complexities of "pure persuasion," involves a meta-poetic as well. But it has to be added at once that Burke's attitude toward poetry is much more positive than Plato's, and his criticism much more congenial and generous.

Excessive systematization is a danger of any elaborate critical theory. Certainly, Burke's "meta-rhetorical" tendency is much less of a temptation than the "fearful symmetry" of Northrop Frye's system or the Aristotelian logical rigor of Elder Olson's critical pluralism. Other dangers implicit in Burke's Dramatistic-logological poetic are: (1) the emphasis on a continuity between artistic and non-artistic activities, at least as far as the idea of tracking down the implications of a terminology is concerned; (2) occasionally still the slighting of some aspects of a work's concrete content, as when the particulars of a character are too summarily treated as the prerequisites of his role; and (3) the slighting of poetic structure in favor of the terminology of the poet.

Yet one must hasten to add the important modification that these are dangers flickering about the edges of Burke's critical theory. In his practical criticism, he properly focuses on the text under inspection; and the reader always comes away with insights into the work which he did not have before—whether he accepts them or quarrels with them. What other end should practical criticism serve?

III *Dramatism as an Epistemic System*

An assessment of Dramatism as a total world view and as a system of inference and knowledge can conveniently be approached by briefly considering three issues: (a) its relation with dialectic; (b) its relation with science; and (c) the implication of "imputing" motives.

(a) *Dramatism and dialectic.* Probably the most searching short discussion of Dramatism is Francis Fergusson's friendly review of the *Grammar of Motives.*[9] In one of his penetrating remarks, he questions the correctness of Burke's identification of Dramatism and dialectic. Defining dialectic as a purely rational pursuit, he implies that in the Platonic dialogues—"certainly the *locus classicus* for the study of the relation between drama and dialectic"—the participants are not affected existentially, and Socrates does not even change intellectually. Drama, on the other hand, and specifically tragedy, subjects man both to a mental and an experiential transformation: Oedipus suffers a new *insight*, and he certainly *suffers* it.

This distinction between the Platonic dialogues and Greek tragedy is unquestionably correct, though in the end even Socrates is victimized. Furthermore, as far as Burke's later logological transformations are concerned, they are indeed Platonic in the sense which Fergusson points out: they are purely intellectual exercises. In many of Burke's later writings, considerations of ritual drama —the pattern of suffering an insight by existential involvement— exist only marginally. In this sense, logology transcends or purifies Dramatism.

In this connection, a passage in a 1952 essay of Burke (somewhat condensed in *Language as Symbolic Action*) is very revealing: while reviewing his progress in writing this book, Burke remarks that his essay on scatological elements in literature, "The Thinking of the Body," had purified his subject so that he could now approach tragedy strictly as a form.[10] Nevertheless, the existential element of ritual tragedy is never wholly eliminated from Burke's later speculations. Nor should it be; for though Fergusson's view of the Platonic dialogues as purely intellectual pursuits conforms to received opinion[11] it is doubtful whether the Platonic dialectic might not need to be supplemented. If it is true that, in the Hegelian and Burkean sense, dialectic is characterized by the necessary exploration of an object in terms of its negation, as a thought process that progresses by encompassing opposites, the highest form of dialectic will also encompass the opposite of the intellect: physical extension, the body. In this sense, it is true that the corrective to all thinking is the body (TBL, 9). Thus, Dramatism is a perfect match to Burke's early estheticism, which had been defined as an intellectual pursuit of anti-intellectualism (cf. above, Chapter 3, Section VI). The Burkean identification of dialectic and drama is a perfect way of expressing this point. The tragic rhythm, according to which one suffers an insight, and which has been so brilliantly adapted by Fergusson, argues against his very own theoretical strictures against Dramatism.

(b) *Dramatism and Science.* Burke's attitude toward science, throughout, has been mixed, to say the least. Though he insists that he has no intention of outlawing it, he has consistently used it as a prime scapegoat. Characteristic of this lesser regard of science—which Burke primarily understands as applied science and technology—is the fact that he assigns to it the realm of sheer *motion*, whereas he makes the claim that Dramatism is the proper discipline to deal with *action*. This alignment involves Burke in difficulties when dealing with empirical reality. For ultimately, Dramatism, and especially its offshoot, logologic, serves to build a self-contained verbal universe with only little contact with the other orders of reality. There are many points where this loss of contact could be observed, but none is perhaps so striking as the following argument from *The Rhetoric of Religion:* Burke is humanistically concerned with defending the notion of free will:

> The logological statement would be "true logologically" even if it were not true ontologically. That is, even if we hypothetically suppose, with strict behaviorists, cyberneticists and the like, that there is no such thing as "free will," that all "action" is reducible to terms of mechanical "motion," it would still remain true that implicit in the idea of action there is the idea of freedom. If one cannot make a choice, one is not acting, one is but being moved, like a billiard ball tapped with a cue and behaving mechanically in conformity with the resistances it encounters. But even if men are doing nothing more than that, the *word* "act" *implies* that they are doing more—and we are now concerned solely with the implications of terms. (RR, 188)

This argument overlooks the fact that the behaviorist, or cyberneticist, theories are scientific hypotheses that permit verification. If they should be proved true, the term "act" would either have to be redefined or dropped altogether, just as the Copernican revolution brought about the radical redefinition of the term "stars" from "holes in the ultimate celestial sphere" to "celestial bodies" and made it imperative to drop such a term as "epicycle" from the terminology describing planetary motions. But the pitting of a scientific claim against Burke's Dramatistic assertion that science is inadequate as a calculus for describing the social and psychological spheres does not solve the issue. The only viable dialectical argument in favor of a scientific modification of Dramatism has to find a fulcrum within Dramatism itself; and a modification of this type would not destroy but expand Dramatism.

There seems to be a possibility for such a delicate operation.

The appropriate point of departure is the Dramatistic alignment, Dramatism versus scientism, or act versus knowledge, or action versus motion. For despite his elaborate and elucidating discussion of the relationship between action and motion in both the *Grammar of Motives* and the *Rhetoric of Motives*, Burke has not yet completely rounded out the cycle of terms implied in "motion." He has not yet fully treated the logologic of the pun on "move." Sheer motion certainly is a strictly physical term; but, on the other hand, there are such views as the traditional definition of the end of rhetoric, "to move to action." Burke touches upon this pun when he refers to man as "moved by the sense of order" (RR, 42n), when he mentions that symbols "move" men (RR, 301), or when he discusses his sense of where "the world is moving towards" politically—a movement within the sphere of action.[12]

Also, as a reviewer has noted, though not without animosity, several of the key terms from the *Grammar of Motives* (placement, position, transformation) are terms of motion, not action.[13] The contention made here is that a further logological analysis of "motion," "move," would make it possible fully to introduce the epistemic (or "scientific," as Burke calls it) element into Dramatism without obliterating its basic Emersonian distinction between laws for men and laws for things. And, while it is fundamentally true that the appropriate approach to people who must be persuaded differs from the appropriate approach to things (which can be manipulated), it is just as true that Dramatism must systematically open itself to the epistemic dimension; it can do so without vitiating its basic insights.

(c) *"Imputing" motives.* These considerations certainly do not imply that Dramatism in its present form has no value. Paradoxically, one of its prime values resides exactly in its skeptical attitude toward a scientific, univocal theory of human conduct. The motivation of a human act is so complex that any scientific theory so far has amounted only to oversimplifying, falsifying reductions. And, even if an ideal scientific calculus of action were devised, it would not be freely applicable outside the laboratory; for human relations do not normally occur under controlled conditions. For these reasons, it seems safe to assume that all the facts will never be available.

This view does not in any way belittle research efforts in the sphere of the *humaniora;* but it suggests why in this area it will always to some extent be necessary to reason from opinion, as Aristotle put it. Similarly, Cardinal Newman recognizes that the guiding principle of human action must operate at a relatively low level of certitude, despite the relatively high value of human action. In Burke's words, it will always be necessary to attribute motives; and in this sense Dramatism, the systematic exploration of the conditions of this "imputation," is a highly commendable humanistic endeavor. Like any philosophy of human conduct, it must to a great extent base the concept of the freedom of human action on opinion, belief; and it can only provide what de Gourmont called "*la illusion de la liberté.*"

But as a humanism, Dramatism should not be slighted. It is true that, considered scientifically, it is open to objections, especially since it is most at home within an almost purely verbal universe. In this sense, it could be viewed as pure poetry. Indeed, Burke's most eloquent and vigorous writing occurs in his imaginative works and in those passages of his argumentative books in which his attitude is more imaginative than argumentative, more erotic in the wise Socratic sense than eristic, disputative. For all these reasons, the Dramatistic-logological theory of literature provides highly congenial tools for the analysis and exegesis of poetic texts which critics can carefully try to use in their own practice.

Aside from this, and considered dramatistically, Dramatism is of great existential importance to its author. For by his "spinning out" of terminological implications, Burke has in a sense become "spun in," too. But this observation implies no censure. It is no mean achievement if the life's work of a man can be summed up in the words humanism, poetry, and wisdom.

CHAPTER 9

Conclusion

IS Dramatism, then, a subjective world view and system of thought unable to stand independent of its author? In answering this question, one should take into account that the personal factor—whether under the name of taste, sensibility, rationalization, or any other—is indeed of much greater importance in the arts and humanities than in the sciences. The latter are characterized by a much more uniform method, which is capable of objective, formulaic statement and a type of verification which enforces consent; hence, it is more easily taught and learned. Given these inevitable differences, Burke's theories have nevertheless been "socialized" to a considerable degree: they have transcended the personal realm by exerting influence on a number of different disciplines. It would not come as a surprise if this influence should spread even further and become more intensive, although literary criticism, social psychology, and the theory of various aspects of language will perhaps continue to be the area in which students profit most from Burke's thought. But Dramatism is so comprehensive that to new readers it may also become suggestive in new ways. What, then, are the main elements of Burke's thought and style? [1]

I *The Anti-Technological Stance of Dramatism*

Basic to Burke's thought and life is an outspoken dislike of progress, technology, machine civilization, and cults of efficiency. In his early work, this attitude is manifest in his radical Bohemianism. It later separated into two strains. One is an agrarian, "metabiological" stance akin to that of Thoreau, the Jeffersonians, and the Populists. In a sense, this attitude is almost Confucian[2] and has, in its extreme, come close to a denunciation of science as a pretext for sadistic rat-torturers. Yet lately Burke has tried to make peace with technology by recommending a neo-Stoical resignation: "For better or worse, men are set to complete the development of technology" (GM, 442).

The second aspect of Burke's anti-scientism is more specifically anti-capitalist and has led him to sympathize with the Communist movement, though his communism was highly individualistic and romantic. One important factor in the attraction that communism had for him was, paradoxically, its collectivism, in which Burke hoped to find the basis for the artistic communication which his esthetic theory required. Burke also hoped to find comic, skeptical, and humanistic elements in communism, but he found instead only humorless, doctrinaire, and dictatorial rigorism. Communism does no longer figure in the *Motivorum Corpus,* though Burke persists in his unorthodox use of some of Marx's ideas.

II *Literature and the Campaign of Living*

Burke's changing attitude toward science indicates a certain degree of acquiescence, though his coming to terms means only an uneasy truce. For, after all, technology heightens the hazards concomitant with life as such. Characteristically, Burke considers art in close complementary relation with hostile life. Threat is the basis of beauty, and literature is a strategy in the campaign of living, an equipment which comforts, an arsenal of arms which protects.

Probably the most important defensive weapon in Burke's arsenal is the attitude of doubt, of irony, of skepticism—the both/and attitude. Counter-stating, corrective discounting, and scrupulosity are all aspects of the same strategy. Whatever the threat may be, Burke has a simultaneous sense of fundamental kinship with the enemy. As he sees it, in satire the author is castigating his own weaknesses and temptations in others (ATH, 49). In this sense, Burke is justified in defining humor as humility and humanization, though it is certain that the mere sound of the words has also contributed to this identification.

III *The Literary Style of Burke's Campaign*

The type of phonetic associationism referred to above is one of the stylistic difficulties and obscurities of Burke's work. Actually, such difficulties are inherent in his subject matter. Concerned as he is with insights that lie on the bias with received categories and departments of thought, interested in the methodology of the pun, in perspectives by incongruity, dialectical logic, the implications of the negative, and in similar subtle speculations, he requires untiring intellectual effort from his readers. Burke never talks down to them; nevertheless, he usually tries to make his arguments palpable by selecting an anecdote as the point of departure of his train of thought and by providing illustrations as he goes along. The reader must not make the mistake of skipping lightly over these seemingly narrative portions of Burke's exposition. They are representative and central.

One of the charges frequently leveled at Burke is the complaint that he is a jargon critic. But what sounds like jargon—and what can become such at times—is his special terminology: "perspective by incongruity," "bureaucratization of the imaginative," "strategy toward a situation." Though cumbersome at times, and always requiring an effort, his terms are hardly ever really obfuscating. Therefore, Burke's satirizing of German idealist philosophers as authors who "write like the shifting of cars in a freight yard" is a roundabout but tongue-in-cheek satire of himself. Nevertheless, even severe critics have conceded that, at his best, Burke writes prose of distinction.

Another stylistic trick which has irritated readers is that of dialectic stress-shifting—the distinction, for instance, between the "verbalization of *experience*" and the "*verbalization* of experience" —yet it is a neat and meaningful device and most effective unless overdone. Burke has also been berated for his liberal use of quotation marks. Hyman defends this practice as a "brilliantly effective device" for emphasis, pointing up double meanings, and marking of special sense. But Burke's use is more complex than that. In addition to the uses which Hyman notes, Burke employs quotation marks as a scrupulous way of indicating borrowings, even when he does not identify the exact source; as a means of dissociating himself from some term or its usage; as a device for transferring or stretching terms, in keeping with planned incongruity; and as a tool for his Benthamite pointing up of the sunken metaphor or unrealized etymology in a term. Though unusual, this practice, as well as the bulk of footnotes which characterizes Burke's books of the 1930's, is immensely suggestive and documents the width of material upon which he draws.

IV *Pun as Epistemic Device*

Burke's most striking figure is the pun. But as he uses it, the pun is much more than a matter of style. He "puts into his puns the heart of what he has to say." [3] This statement requires amplification. For Burke's central technique of planned incongruity is itself to a large extent the methodology of the pun; though Burke speaks of the possibility of using rational, intellectual puns, *tonal* puns serve as important links in all of his works. Thus, his aphorism, "Watch the mind as you would eye a mean dog," is certainly supported by the tonal correspondence, *mind—mean d*og.

The methodology of the pun also serves to reveal hidden or forbidden meanings in imaginative literature. To support his Freudian view of an *ecclesia super cloacam,* he discovers an Anglo-French pun in Eliot's title, *"Murder" in the Cathedral;* by ablaut, metathesis, and substitution of cognates, he extracts a similar scatological meaning from Keats's line, "Beauty is Truth, Truth Beauty. . . ." Burke's concern with such unsavory matters increased in his later work and has led him to the conception of a "Demonic Trinity" (the functions of the *pudenda* lumped together as excretory or expressive) and the systematic search for the "Thinking of the Body," for catharsis in terms of fecal images (LSA, 308–43). It should be added that his pun analysis is not exclusively scatology-oriented and that he does not offer these psychoanalytical reductions as the essence of the work (RM, 279), as analysts usually do, but sees them as potent ambiguities (RM, 322).

These concerns have a central place in Burke's theories because they also have a vital existential meaning for him. By way of the scatology-eschatology pun (RM, 308) and his association of the anal-offal with death (RM, 263, 371n), making peace with the feces is a business and a duty of paramount importance for him. The question is to what extent such an elaborate pun analysis can have an epistemic function. Under the trade name of "joycing" (constituting a bilingual pun on Freud?), Burke has made ample use of it in his criticism. Since, however, Joyce does his twisting and forcing of words primarily in the service of imaginative literature, it might be better to rename the pun analysis in criticism and call it "burking." Turning this method on the very name of its author, W. S. Knickerbocker has identified Kenneth Burke as the man who "knows what is under bourgeois society" (*kens* what is be*neath* the *burg*).[4] Other possibilities suggest themselves, also in other areas: in the light of Burke's scatological interests, his insistence on a special way of "analogical" thinking readily lends itself to a "burking" treatment by teaming it with the later term "logology," which develops from the former and is contiguous with it. The pair evokes the mystical design of the uroboros, the snake which bites its own tail—one of Burke's emblems of his concept of the mystery of hierarchy. This idea seems to be implicitly contained in the pun on "faces" which he had used in one of his early poems, "Atlantis" (BM, 61).

With a little patience and practice, it would be possible to spin out further possibilities, "symbolic" shortcuts among Burke's terms. They would, perhaps, testify to the critic's ingenuity; expertly handled, they could reveal much about the functioning of Burke's mind. But unrestrained "burking" or "joycing" may easily spin out of control by losing contact with the hard surface of the text. It must be credited to Burke's good sense and sensibility that most of his recent critical studies of individual works avoid the cryptological excesses to which this method lends itself in principle.

V *Dramatism as Transcendence of Psychoanalysis Toward Language-Analysis*

The Freudian basis of all these speculations is evident. Burke heavily relies on Freud, although he has made important reservations and never applied psychoanalysis to the symbol-mongering kind of paraphrasing poems. Burke transcended Freudianism by extending its categories such as coercive selection, distortion, condensation, displacement, and so on, to language as a whole. Freud's "dream work" becomes Burke's "language work." As he sees it, language in general, not only in its idiosyncratic private uses but in every single one of its specialized technical variants—physicist, sociological, psychological, poetic, and others—serves as so many "terministic screens" which select and deflect reality as they reflect it (LSA, 51–52, 66).

This diagnosis of Burke's increasing concern with language, with the erection of a purely verbal empire, is also corroborated by other evidence. His early psychosomatic Platonism becomes strikingly linguistic in the recent theory of "entitlement" (LSA, 373, 378–79). One may also note the Platonic nature of his dialectic which, unlike the Hegelian and Marxist, is not concerned with any progression in time but with the construction of a terminological hierarchy—or, rather, four hierarchies: the natural, the verbal, the socio-economico-political, and the supernatural, with the verbal as the "foremost among the equals" (LSA, 375).

VI *Animal* Naturaliter Christianum

If language has become the foundation of Burke's system, it has done so by merging with a basic religious orientation which has characterized his thought and writing from the beginning. This assertion is not in the least intended to preempt Burke for any religious denomination; it does, however, recognize that, in erecting his system, he has widely and intensely drawn upon religious experience and theological forms of thought. He has defined psychoanalysis as "secular conversion"; he agrees with Marston's identification of Freud's hypothesis of the latent abnormality of everyone as a secular variant of the Christian doctrine of original sin; he has recommended his own attempt at a transvaluation of values as analogous to the rise of Christianity. On the verbal level, Burke has acted as the good shepherd of lost words. Throughout his works, he has taken words in bad repute, such as "scapegoat," "rationalization," "hysteria," "rhetoric," or disregarded philosophical concepts such as that of substance, and tried to lead them back into the fold of respectable usage.

Apart from these details, the over-all religious orientation of Dramatism-logology is also evident. W. H. Rueckert hardly overstates the case when he observes: "The whole dramatistic system is laid out on a moral-ethical, Christian-Catholic bias, and is presented in such a way as to make perfectly clear Burke's belief that he has developed a new 'scientific' religion which twentieth-century man can 'believe' in, but which, unlike the old one it replaces, is designed to save man in this world." [5] Concessions to the modern temper are his reduction of God to a dialectical god-term in the sense of the Platonic *to kalon,* the recognition of heaven and hell as psychological states, and others.

VII *The Beautiful and the Good*

On the basis of these considerations, a final concise definition of Burke's critical stand is possible. The philosophy of art appropriate to Dramatism, the world view that goes through good and evil beyond good and evil, is one in which the esthetic and the ethical merge. Yet there is no stocky moralism in Burke. The ethical, in the sense which Burke shares with Aristotle, is the act of choice, though with a difference of emphasis: Burke's pragmatist orientation leads him to regard choice primarily as the selection of *means.* "Morality" enters in the sense that, for Burke, the good life is characterized by an intensive experience of intense esthetic moments, an experience which for him sublimates all the aggressiveness that is at the root of existence. This attitude which "purifies war" inspires the *Motivorum Corpus* whose motto is, *ad bellum purificandum.* At the same time, the emphasis on the ethical *qua* decision rules out any connection of Burke's view of life with insipid pleasure-seeking.

If the predominant modern critical orientation, in the Romantic and post-Romantic tradition, regards poetry primarily as based on a conjunction of the first two members of the classical triad—beauty, truth, and the good—(Keats, Baudelaire, Rilke, and the early Eliot at once come to mind as representative shapers and users of this beauty-truth pair as one of the crucial elements in their poetry and their poetics) Burke stands apart: in all aspects of esthetic theory, as well as of his systematic thought, he stresses the beautiful and the good.

The beautiful and the good, wisdom, poetry, humanism—these are categories that characterize the life and work of Kenneth Burke. As he sees it, all these concerns are ultimately rooted in, and merge with, language. Thus, Dramatism-logology, as one form of a secularization of religion, can perhaps best be summed up by re(?)translating the first Logological sentence from the temporal into the essential: *in principio est verbum.* Basically the same idea is expressed in a much less solemn tone in one of Burke's own little hortatory poems:

> The Word is a snare,
> It lurks as in a lare.
>
> The Word is a sneer.
> It jeers as with a leer.
>
> The Word can inspire,
> It sings as with a lyre.
>
> The Word is store and cure,
> Study its lore and lure.
> (CP, 233)

Notes and References

Chapter One

1. Cf. M. Josephson, *Life Among the Surrealists* (New York, 1962), p. 35.

2. Cf. the first clause of Burke's "Definition of Man" (1963), *Language as Symbolic Action: Essays on Life, Literature, and Method* (Berkeley & Los Angeles, 1966), pp. 3–9; subsequently cited as LSA.

3. With his successful translation of some of Mann's stories (notably *Death in Venice*, New York, 1925), Burke later contributed substantially to Mann's reception in the United States. He also translated parts of O. Spengler's *The Decline of the West* for *The Dial*.

4. Quoted in M. Cowley, *Exile's Return* (2nd. enl. ed., New York, 1951), pp. 20–21.

5. W. Wasserstrom, *The Time of "The Dial"* (Syracuse, N. Y., 1963). Wasserstrom is, however, in error when he states that the reference to Burke in Miss Moore's poem, "Picking and Choosing," is to Kenneth (p. 114); it is to Edmund Burke (cf. her *Observations* [New York, 1924], Index). In a sense it can, of course, be taken to apply to both (cf. R. P. Blackmur, *The Double Agent* [New York, 1935], p. 293).

6. *Permanence and Change: An Anatomy of Purpose* (rev. ed., Los Altos, Calif., 1954), p. 5; subsequently cited as PC.

7. This is not to say that *The Dial* was but a successor of *The Seven Arts*. For a critical discussion of their relationship cf. G. A. M. Janssens, *The American Literary Review: A Critical History 1920–1950* (The Hague, 1968), pp. 39–51.

8. The references are to an uncharitable article by Ernest Boyd in *The American Mercury*, I (January, 1924), 51–56, and a prankish reply by Burke and his friends in the form of a single-issue magazine, *Aesthete 1925*, I (February, 1925).

9. *American Writers' Congress*, ed. H. Hart (London [1936]), pp. 87–94; for the discussion, cf. pp. 167–71; cf. also D. Aaron, *Writers on the Left* (New York, 1961), pp. 283–92.

10. W. S. Knickerbocker, "Wam for Maw," *The Sewanee Review*, XLIX (October–December, 1941), 535.

Chapter Two

1. K. Burke, *The White Oxen and Other Stories* (New York, 1924), p. 62; subsequently quoted as WO. *The Complete White Oxen: Collected Short Fiction of Kenneth Burke* (Berkeley & Los Angeles, 1968) is enlarged by four stories. Some juvenile fiction remains uncollected.

2. C. H. Grattan, untitled review, *The Literary Digest,* III (December, 1924), 60.

3. Cf. M. Josephson, "Experimental," *Books* (N.Y. *Herald Tribune*), LXXXIV (November 16, 1924), 4.

4. Cf. G. B. Munson, "An Amazing Debut," *The Literary Review* (N. Y. *Evening Post*), V (October 11, 1924), 3; cf. also his "In and About the Workshop of Kenneth Burke," *The Calendar* (London), III (July, 1926), esp. 135.

5. Cf. M. Cowley, "Gulliver," *The Dial,* LXXVII (December, 1924), esp. 521.

6. Cf. A. Warren, "Kenneth Burke: His Mind and Art," *The Sewanee Review,* XLI (1933), 225–36, 344–64; Warren proposes a fourfold division: (a) true to life; (b) the realistic *cum* fantastic; (c) purely non-realistic stories; (d) stories "concerned with the sort of persons and scenes and situations commonly dealt with by realistic techniques but introducing expressionistic elements" (p. 231).

7. 1925; repr. in K. Burke, *Counter-Statement* (New York, 1931); for a more detailed analysis, cf. below, Chapter 3; subsequently cited as CS from the second edition (Los Altos, Calif., 1953).

8. The term is Flaubert's; for a concise explanation, though with the emphasis on the author, cf. W. C. Booth, *The Rhetoric of Fiction* (Chicago, 1961), pp. 81–83.

9. On the requirement of an intrinsic relation between *significans* and *significatum,* cf. R. Wellek and A. Warren, *Theory of Literature* (London, 1955), p. 193.

10. "Scene-act ratio" is Burke's term for the relationship between an act and its context (cf. *A Grammar of Motives,* New York, 1945, esp. p. 7; subsequently cited as GM). Thus, in plays of symbolic realism, the scene or stage set may foreshadow, or implicitly contain, the action.

11. *The Works of Edgar Allan Poe* (New York, 1848, vol. III), pp. 192–93.

12. Cf. Cowley, "Gulliver," p. 521.

13. M. Ernst, *Oeuvres de 1919 à 1936* (Paris, 1937), p. 31; English translation in *Beyond Painting* (New York, 1948), p. 13. The subsequent quotations are from this translation.

14. Cf. esp. R. de Gourmont, *La Culture des Idées* (12th ed., Paris, 1916), pp. 69–79.

15. Cf. *The Literary Essays of Ezra Pound*, ed. T. S. Eliot (2nd ed., London, 1960), p. 3. Cf. my discussion of the image in Imagist theory and practice, "Das Bild in imagistischer Theorie und Praxis," *Jahrbuch für Amerikastudien*, XIII (1968), 174–95.

16. ". . . the self becomes a bundle of minor animosities, and is defined by its surface irritations and reflexes of combative dissent." Anon., "Psychological Drama," *Book Review* (N.Y. *Times*), LXXIV (October 26, 1924), 26.

17. A conflicting opinion is expressed by W. Seitz. Accordingly, Ernst's later work has "relinquished the physical and structural basis of collage," exactly because of its finish and homogeneity (*The Art of Assemblage* [Garden City, N.Y., 1961] p. 41). Such a view is justified from the art historian's perspective. But since Seitz, following J. Dubuffet, introduces the term *assemblage* for pictorial works in the mainstream of this tradition, it is admissible to follow Ernst and Breton in dissociating "collage" from its etymological meaning and to apply it to figurative collations and related techniques in other artistic media.

18. "Un procédé absolument analogue à celui de l'image poétique," L. Aragon, *Les Collages* (Paris, 1965), p. 30.

19. Cf. esp. A. Rimbaud, *Une Saison en Enfer* (Paris, 1946), pp. 70–71 (written in 1873). J. Laforgue's "contaminations" such as "éternullité," "éléphantaisiste," etc., are also in this tradition.

20. "Beautiful . . . like the chance encounter of a sewing-machine and an umbrella upon a dissecting table," *Les Chants de Maldoror* (Paris-Bruxelles, 1874), pp. 289–90.

21. Cf. also K. Burke, *Book of Moments: Poems 1915–1954* (Los Altos, Calif., 1955), p. 93; subsequently cited as BM. With identical pagination, BM forms the first part of *Collected Poems 1915–1967* (Berkeley & Los Angeles, 1968); subsequently cited as CP.

22. Cf. also K. Burke, *Terms for Order*, ed. S. E. Hyman (Bloomington, Ind., 1964), p. 147; subsequently cited as TO.

23. Letter by Mr. Burke to author, February 11, 1966.

24. In discussing the "Thinking of the Body," Burke finds a scatological meaning in the ending of "Quest" (LSA, 336–38). In so doing, he relies upon childhood memories which the reader is unable to infer from the text. Burke's regressive exegesis is thus couched in terms of private psychology; the present interpretation emphasizes the progressive structure of the story as it is accessible for common psychology.

Chapter Three

1. Although the word "scandal" occurs in an elaborate comparison, the whole example does, of course, refer to the situation of the Danes.

2. L. T. Lemon exaggerates his just criticism of this point by overemphasizing the function of intrinsic interest. Cf. *The Partial Critics* (New York, 1965), pp. 172–76.

3. W. H. Rueckert, *Kenneth Burke and the Drama of Human Relations* (Minneapolis, 1963), p. 10. But only the chapter on CS is static in this sense; Rueckert's over-all approach quite properly emphasizes the developmental aspect of Burke's literary theory and criticism.

4. Cf. R. W. B. Lewis, "Lionel Trilling and the New Stoicism," *The Hudson Review,* III (Summer, 1950), 313–17; L. Gallino, "Kenneth Burke e la Critica Americana," *Studi Americani,* III (1957), esp. 326–30; R. Wellek, "Literaturkritik und Literaturwissenschaft," *Lexicon der Modernen Weltliteratur* (Freiburg, 1961), vol. II, esp. column 226.

5. This is the purpose of Burke's work beginning with GM: to devise a "lingua Adamica" which comprehends the universe of man's intellective and imaginative activity, his "symbolicity." He also frequently recommends neo-Stoicism; cf. his *Attitudes toward History* (rev. ed., Los Altos, Calif., 1954 only), esp. p. 358; subsequently cited as ATH; cf. also GM, 442.

6. CS, 105. The argument, though not the term "body dogmatic" is Burke's. One element of this inherent contradiction can be recognized in the fact that, despite this programmatic repudiation of the body, "form," the central category of the esthetic of CS, is based exactly on such somatic requirements; cf. below, pp. 52, 62.

7. Cf. L. Trilling, *The Liberal Imagination: Essays on Literature and Society* (New York, 1950), pp. xiii, xv and *passim.*

8. In this context it becomes clear that the more or less antagonistically worded objections to Burke's "pure aestheticism," to his single standard of technique, which were made by some of the early reviewers, fall short of a full grasp of his theory. Cf. esp. G. B. Munson, "Debut"; G. Hicks, "A Defense of Eloquence," *The New Republic,* LXIX (December 2, 1931), 75–76.

9. Cf. W. Pater, *The Renaissance* (London, 1900), p. viii.

10. De Gourmont is certainly not the inventor of this attitude or of symbolism but a critic who, in a central part of his encyclopedic system of thought, furnished a rationale of it. His influence on British and American critics and poets was great. Cf. G. S. Burne, *Remy de Gourmont: His Ideas and Influence in England and America* (Carbondale & Edwardsville, Ill., 1963), esp. pp. 111–53.

11. R. de Gourmont, *Culture*, p. 4; my translation.
12. *Ibid.*, pp. 69–106.
13. The question whether Burke's theory of form provides a basis for literary judgment was violently debated in most of the reviews. I. Schneider (*Books*, N.Y. *Herald Tribune*, VIII [December 13, 1931], 4), recognizing the parallels between Burke's and Richards' endeavors, asserted that CS provides a sane, sure, useful standard of judgment. Hicks ("Defense") also conceded that the principles of CS rendered literary judgment possible, though he rejected them as purely technical. H. Rosenberg (*Symposium*, III [January, 1932], 116–20), however, finds that CS offers psychology instead of judgment, universals instead of particulars, and that its principles are undiscriminating. This objection was to be raised again and again, e.g., by Blackmur, *Double Agent*, p. 294. Yet all this quibbling would have been unnecessary had the critics recognized that Burke did not intend to provide an automatic standard for evaluating literary works but "an instrument for clarifying critical issues" (CS, ix)—which is quite a different type of judgment.
14. Thus, when E. E. Stoll concluded that Shakespeare "observes not so much the probabilities of the action or the psychology of the character, but the psychology of the audience, for whom both action and character are framed" (*Art and Artifice in Shakespeare* [Cambridge, England, 1933], p. 168), Burke had already developed his own independent insight into this matter and had based an esthetic theory upon this observation.
15. ". . . the technique and the personal interest, bound up tightly and contending all but equally; the strain of contraries, the not quite resolvable dualism, that is art." J. C. Ransom, *The World's Body* (1939; repr. Port Washington, N.Y., 1964), p. 4.
16. K. Burke, "The Poetic Process," *The Guardian*, II (May–June, 1925), 281–94; "Psychology and Form," *The Dial*, LXXIX (July, 1925), 34–46.
17. In discussing Burke's concept of form, it is absolutely essential to stick by the term *aspects* to describe the variants; for they are not mutually exclusive: in fact, some of the most powerful artistic effects result from the intermingling of "forms." It is therefore false in more than one way to paraphrase Burke as distinguishing "three kinds of rhetorical structure . . . repetitive, progressive, and syllogistic" (F. Murphy, ed., *Discussions of Poetry: Form and Structure* [Boston, 1964], p. vii).
18. This reader-oriented esthetic implies that literary perfection does not exist because there is no perfect reader (CS, 178–79). The closest approximation to this ideal, Burke feels, is the "hypothetical norm" of the connoisseur. While all other kinds of readers are "hys-

terical" in that each of them categorically requires "one very specific kind of art . . . 'medicinal' to his situation," the connoisseur will approach *all* Symbols *as art,* "thus requiring the maximum of ritualization, verbalization," of eloquence, rhetoric (CS, 180). But are readers really so "hysterical" as Burke assumes, really so absolute in their preferences? If they *are,* then the connoisseur is less catholic than it might appear: he is the type of reader that is "hysterical" about rhetoric; if they *aren't,* it is not necessary to postulate the ideal connoisseur.

19. Cf. I. A. Richards, *Principles of Literary Criticism* (London, 1960), pp. 225–27.

20. Cf. Wellek-Warren, *Theory,* p. 147.

21. Y. Winters, explicitly referring to CS, distinguishes seven "structural methods" (*In Defense of Reason* [3rd ed., Denver, n.d.], pp. 30–74). There are important differences between Winters' structuralism and Burke's formalism as far as the conceptual frame is concerned. Whereas Burke's view of the matter is audience-regarding (formula: audience psychology = emotion = technique = *aspects* of form), Winters' is author-oriented (author morality = feeling = technique = categorical *method* of structure).

22. Cf. S. E. Hyman, *The Tangled Bank* (New York, 1962), p. 361.

23. First printed in *Die Philosophie der Literaturwissenschaft,* ed. E. Ermatinger (Berlin, 1929); English in *Modern Man in Search of His Soul* (New York, 1933).

24. Cf. for instance N. Frye, *Anatomy of Criticism* (Princeton, N.J., 1957), pp. 4–5. Frye differs from Burke insofar as he insists on the view that the poet does not *address* an audience. Cf. also A. MacLeish's poem "Ars Poetica."

25. "Beauty is characterized by the sensuous appearance/resplendence of the idea." (F. W. Hegel, *Sämtliche Werke,* XII [Stuttgart, 1937], 160.) The pun on "Schein" (appearance and resplendence) actually rules out a simplistic doctrinaire interpretation of this passage.

Chapter Four

1. K. Burke, *Towards a Better Life, Being a Series of Epistles, or Declamations* (2nd ed., Berkeley & Los Angeles, 1966), p. 219; pagination identical with original ed.; subsequently cited as TBL.

2. I. Schneider, *The Bookman,* LXXV (April, 1932), 102.

3. M. Cowley, "Unwilling Novelist," *The New Republic,* LXX (February 17, 1932), 23.

4. Cf. T. Mann, "Tod in Venedig," *Sämtliche Erzählungen* (Frank-

furt, 1963), p. 358; K. Burke, "Thomas Mann and André Gide," CS, 92.

5. The apt title of R. Cantwell's review, *The Nation*, CXXXIV (March 9, 1932), 289.

6. "What Burke has done is, I believe, to effect this segregation of a part of his inner life and to invent for it a *symbol*, a *myth*, in the shape of a fiction, a series of events calculated to give manifestations of this inner life." A. Warren, "Burke," 347–48.

7. "Unwilling Novelist," *loc. cit.*

8. Cf. J. Chamberlain, "Mr. Burke's Experiment in the Novel," *Book Review* (N.Y. *Times*), LXXX (January 31, 1932), 2.

9. Cf. D. Barnes, *Nightwood* (Norfolk, Conn., 1961), esp. p. xii.

Chapter Five

1. PC "contains more sound substance than any text on social psychology with which the reviewer is familiar." L. Wirth, *American Journal of Sociology*, XLIII (November, 1937), 483; C. W. Mills recommends Burke's method of planned incongruity as an ideal source of sociological insight. Cf. his *The Sociological Imagination* (New York, 1954), p. 215, n. 5.

2. Cf. A. Warren, "Sceptic's Progress," *American Review*, VI (December, 1935), 201.

3. Successively, the quotations are from: R. Cantwell, *New Outlook*, CLXV (June, 1935), 58; H. Rosenberg, "Meaning and Communication," *Poetry*, XLVII (March, 1936), 347; E. S. Bates, "A Spendthrift with Ideas," *Books* (N.Y. *Herald Tribune*), XI (May 12, 1935), 8.

4. Later, Burke came to regard these three schemes as simultaneous resources of language as such (PC, xxv). In fact, the emphasis on a philosophy of being with which PC concludes prepares the ground for such a non-historic, synchronic view.

5. The reference to communism (pp. 93–94 of the 1935 ed.) has been excised from the later editions on the ground that it was prompted by the conditions of the 1930's and is not an integral part of the argument (PC, xv).

6. J. Frazer, *The Golden Bough: A Study in Magic and Religion*, I (abr. ed., London, 1960), 65.

7. K. Burke, *A Rhetoric of Motives* (New York, 1950), p. 43; subsequently cited as RM.

8. ATH is "more solid and nourishing than many of the longer and more pretentious philosophies of history now on the market." C. Brinton, "What Is History?" *Saturday Review of Literature*, XVI (August 14, 1937), 3.

9. S. G. Nichols ascribes the term "perspective by incongruity" to R. Wellek (cf. Introduction to Wellek's *Concepts of Criticism,* ed. S. G. Nichols [New Haven, 1963], p. xiv). Yet there is perhaps no other term and concept which is so much Burke's own. In the passage to which Nichols refers, Wellek uses the term in connection with Edward Bullough's definition of "psychical distance" (the "sudden view of things from their reverse, usually unnoticed side"—which comes close to Burke's view). He illustrates the term by referring to theories of novelty in *poetry,* such as Pound's. (In *Theory of Literature,* he names many others, cf. pp. 252–53.) In this connection, he also refers to Brecht's *Verfremdung* (*Concepts,* p. 318), which is, however, rather based on a theory of *acting* (cf. B. Brecht, *Schriften zum Theater* [Frankfurt, 1960], pp. 76–77). Burke's use of the term is distinct from both: it has an *epistemological* reference.

10. Burke noted the similarity of perspective by incongruity with Surrealist and Dadaist techniques (PC, 112).

11. Note the transference of the principle of "art to reveal art" (CS) from the esthetic to the speculative realm.

12. Burke freely acknowledges his indebtedness to C. K. Ogden and I. A. Richards' *The Meaning of Meaning* (1923) and their criticism of language. But in statements such as this, he actually reverses the recommendations based on their conclusions. Whereas Richards recognizes, with Burke, that metaphors are essential even to scientific discourse (cf. *The Philosophy of Rhetoric,* 2nd ed. [New York, 1965], p. 92), he nevertheless insists on the fact that we "must translate more of our skill into discussable science . . . raise our implicit recognitions into explicit distinctions" (*ibid.,* pp. 94–95), thereby transcending, as best as we can, the metaphorical element. In this connection, it is characteristic that Ogden-Richards use the term "symbolic" to denote the scientific, referential use of language, which in principle is "neutral," whereas Burke's use of the term refers to the emotional, attitudinal, "poetic" use of language (cf. below, p. 96). This shift of emphasis is in keeping with his rejection of Bentham's quest for a neutral terminology (PC, 75–76). Burke's emphasis on language as hortatory, as a means of inducing attitudes, is rather in keeping with B. Malinowski's Supplement to Ogden-Richards' book.

13. For a concise summary of a realistic concept of analogy, cf. F. Fergusson, *The Idea of a Theater* (Princeton, 1949), Appendix.

14. For a variant of this observation, cf. W. Sutton, *Modern American Criticism* (Englewood Cliffs, N.J., 1963), p. 81.

Chapter Six

1. K. Burke, "Revolutionary Symbolism," H. Hart, *Congress*, p. 92.
2. Cf. I. A. Richards, *Principles*, pp. 266–68.
3. Cf. J. Dewey, *Art as Experience* (New York, 1958), esp. pp. 15–16.
4. Cf. K. Burke, *The Philosophy of Literary Form: Studies in Symbolic Action* (2nd ed., Baton Rouge, La., 1967), p. 145; subsequently cited as PLF.
5. Introduction to PC, 1965 ed., p. xv.
6. Cf. A. Gomme, *Attitudes to Criticism* (Carbondale & Edwardsville, Ill., 1966), p. 59.
7. Cf. *ibid.*, pp. 64–65.
8. While in the Freud essay he had rejected non-theological, naturalistic simplifications as oversimplifications (PLF, 262), he now feels that "any simplification is open to the *charge* of 'oversimplification'" (PLF, 22; italics mine). Later, he will accept oversimplification as the rule of any explanatory procedure because any explanation depends on a terminology that simplifies its subject according to its "terministic screen" (LSA, 44–62).
9. Cf. H. Read, *Collected Essays in Literary Criticism* (London, 1948), pp. 59, 60, 67; here, Read discusses the long poem. In his view of the lyric, he is much closer to Burke's attitudinal theory (cf. p. 58).
10. Wellek-Warren, *Theory*, p. 141; italics mine.
11. C. Brooks, *The Well-Wrought Urn* (New York, 1947), p. 195.
12. Cf. esp. the concluding "ontological" chapter of J. C. Ransom's *The New Criticism* (Norfolk, Conn., 1941).
13. "Ein dumpfer schöpferischer Keim." G. Benn, "Probleme der Lyrik," *Gesammelte Werke*, I (Wiesbaden, 1959), 506; note also: "Ein Gedicht ist immer die Frage nach dem Ich"—a poem is always a quest for the self, for identity; *ibid.*, pp. 501–2.
14. T. S. Eliot, *On Poetry and Poets* (London, 1957), p. 98. Subsequently cited as OPP.
15. Burke distinguishes three levels of imagery: the bodily or private level involving kinaesthetic (gripping, repelling, eating) and sensory imagery (decay, drought, ice, etc.); the personal, intimate, familiar, familistic level (overlapping with sensory imagery); and the abstract level involving the placement into larger groups (PLF, 36–37). In ATH, the corresponding terms were: the mimetic, the intimate or childhood, and the abstract, forensic, or adult levels (ATH, 340–41).

16. Cf. R. Flatter, *Hamlet's Father* (New Haven, Conn., 1949), pp. 104–7.

17. It is a remarkable coincidence that Eliot concludes his description of the poetic act in the accents of rejection or disavowal: the poet finally "can say to the poem: 'Go away! Find a place for yourself in a book—and don't expect *me* to take any further interest in you.'" *On Poetry*, p. 98.

18. M. Bewley, "Kenneth Burke as Literary Critic," *Scrutiny*, XV (December, 1948), 254–77.

19. In *The Structure of Complex Words* (1952), Empson "engages rather in a special kind of lexicography than in literary criticism." R. Wellek, *Concepts*, p. 59. The same holds true of his earlier criticism. Cf. E. Olson's essay in *Critics and Criticism, Ancient and Modern*, ed. R. S. Crane (Chicago, 1952), pp. 45–82.

20. T. S. Eliot, *Selected Essays* (3rd enl. ed., London, 1951), p. 32.

21. "The poems of T. E. Hulme only needed to be read aloud to have immediate effect." *Ibid.*

22. A. Tate's concept of "tension in poetry" is more general and abstract than Burke's, though occasionally it contracts into the notion of a polar relationship as when Tate sums up the insight of Marvell's "To His Coy Mistress" in terms of a "conflict of sensuality and asceticism" (*The Man of Letters in the Modern World* [Cleveland & New York, 1955], p. 72); but even this alignment is abstracted from the concrete details of the poem.

23. K. Burke, "Waste—the Future of Prosperity," *The New Republic*, LXXIII (July, 1930), 228–31.

24. Cf. also Quintilian, *Institutes*, VIII. vi. 21.

25. H. P. Guth, "Threat as the Basis of Beauty: Pragmatic Elements in the Aesthetics of Richards, Dewey, and Burke," unpubl. Ph.D. diss., University of Michigan, 1956, p. 261.

26. C. Brooks, *Urn*, p. 195. There are indications that Burke later began to reconsider his views on this matter. A 1964 essay in which he discusses, among other things, the fact that the words "image," "imagination," and "imitation" are derived from a root meaning "like" in the prepositional sense, abruptly and mysteriously ends with the observation: "However, as Coleridge points out, 'imitation' in the poetic sense also involves an explicit awareness of 'unlikeness.'" ("The Unburned Bridges of Poetics, or, How Keep Poetry Pure?" *The Centennial Review*, VIII [Fall, 1964], 397).

27. K. Burke, "The Problem of the Intrinsic" (1942–43), GM, 469.

28. Cf. the basic argument of Burke's "Poetic and Semantic Meaning" (PLF, 138–67); also, LSA, 502.

29. G. Stein, *Three Lives* (New York, 1933), p. 11.

Chapter Seven

1. "We might define the lyric as a poem which embodies a single or simple emotional attitude." H. Read, *Essays*, p. 58.
2. Most of Burke's later poems are "moments," too. They expand topics and techniques developed earlier. It is, therefore, possible to treat them in close connection with his earlier ones. CP consists of three parts: BM (pagination identical with original ed.); "Introduction to What: Poems 1955–1967" (the title is that of the introductory long poem); and "Conclusion."
3. K. Burke, "La Baudelairienne," *The Sansculotte,* I (January, 1917), 9.
4. Title of Burke's first published essay in *Contact* (probably no. 3 of early series, 1920–23), p. 9.
5. G. P. Meyer, "The Enemy of Bureaucracy," *Saturday Review of Literature,* XXXVIII (September 3, 1955), 28.
6. Cf. W. James, *Pragmatism and Other Essays* (New York, 1963), p. 22.
7. M. Moore, "A Grammarian of Motives," *Poetry London–New York,* I (Winter, 1956), 49–52.
8. W. C. Blum, "A Poetry of Perspectives," *Poetry,* LXXXVII (March, 1956), 366.

Chapter Eight

1. In 1962, Burke expands the pentad into a hexad by adding "attitude"—incipient act (GM, 1962 ed., 443–44).
2. K. Burke, "Symbol and Association," *The Hudson Review,* IX (Summer, 1956), 212.
3. Cf. Ogden-Richards, *Meaning,* pp. 313–15.
4. Cf. esp. "How to Make Our Ideas Clear," C. S. Peirce, *Philosophical Writings,* ed. J. Buchler (New York, 1955), pp. 23–41.
5. Cf. F. Fergusson, *The Idea of a Theater* (Princeton, 1949), esp. p. 18.
6. K. Burke, *The Rhetoric of Religion: Studies in Logology* (Boston, 1961); subsequently cited as RR.
7. K. Burke, "Dramatic Form—And: Tracking Down Implications," *Tulane Drama Review,* X (Summer, 1966), 54–63.
8. The other clauses of Burke's definition of man are: inventor of the negative; separated from his natural condition by instruments of his own making; goaded by the spirit of hierarchy (less dramatically put: moved by a sense of order); and rotten with perfection.

9. Cf. F. Fergusson, *The Human Image in Dramatic Literature* (Garden City, N.Y., 1957), pp. 193–204.

10. K. Burke, "Form and Persecution in the *Oresteia,*" *The Sewanee Review,* IX (July–September, 1952), 379; LSA, 126–27.

11. The Platonic dialogues are *not* the classical text for Dramatism, for they lack the "evidence of the action, and the arbitrement of the event." J. C. Ransom, "An Address to Kenneth Burke," *The Kenyon Review,* IV (Spring, 1942), 219–37.

12. Cf. K. Burke, "Motion, Action, Words," *Teachers College Record,* LXII (December, 1960), 248; also, GM, 286.

13. Cf. I. Rosenfeld, *An Age of Enormity* (Cleveland, 1962), p. 164.

Chapter Nine

1. This conclusion overlaps in part with S. E. Hyman's summary of Burke's criticism as presented in *The Armed Vision: A Study of the Methods of Modern Literary Criticism* (New York, 1955), pp. 376–85.

2. Cf. H. B. Parkes, *The Pragmatic Test: Essays on the History of Ideas* (San Francisco, 1941), p. 215.

3. Hyman, *Vision,* p. 383.

4. W. S. Knickerbocker, "Wam for Maw," pp. 534–35; he has also explored other possibilities.

5. Rueckert, *Burke,* pp. 133–34.

Selected Bibliography

This bibliography is rigorously selective in all parts except the sections listing books by and about Burke. Since many of Burke's books are collections of previously published material or contain such material in appendices, his total work is well represented by his books and a small selection from the uncollected items. This bibliography does not, however, reflect his music criticism, his translations, and his numerous reviews. For comprehensive checklists, see "Bibliographies" in Secondary Sources, below.

PRIMARY SOURCES

1. *Books*

The White Oxen and Other Stories. New York: A. & C. Boni, 1924.

Counter-Statement. New York: Harcourt, Brace & Co., 1931; Los Altos, Calif.: Hermes Publications, 1953; Chicago: University of Chicago Press, 1957; Berkeley and Los Angeles: University of California Press, 1968. Collection of critical essays.

Towards a Better Life, Being a Series of Epistles, or Declamations. New York: Harcourt, Brace & Co., 1932; Berkeley and Los Angeles: University of California Press, 1966. Novel.

Permanence and Change: An Anatomy of Purpose. New York: New Republic, Inc., 1935; rev. ed., Los Altos, Calif.: Hermes Publications, 1954; New York: Bobbs-Merrill, 1965.

Attitudes toward History. 2 vols. New York: New Republic, Inc., 1937; rev. one-vol. ed., Los Altos, Calif.: Hermes Publications, 1959; Boston: Beacon Press, 1961.

The Philosophy of Literary Form: Studies in Symbolic Action. Baton Rouge: Louisiana State University Press, 1941, 1967; rev. abr. ed., New York: Vintage, 1957. Collection of critical essays.

A Grammar of Motives. New York: Prentice-Hall, 1945; London: D. Dobson, 1947; New York: G. Braziller, 1955.

A Rhetoric of Motives. New York: Prentice-Hall, 1950; G. Braziller,

1955; together with the *Grammar*, New York: The World Publishing Co., 1962. Philosophy, criticism.

Book of Moments: Poems 1915–1954. Los Altos, Calif.: Hermes Publications, 1955.

The Rhetoric of Religion: Studies in Logology. Boston: Beacon Press, 1961.

Terms for Order and Perspectives by Incongruity. Ed. Stanley E. Hyman. Bloomington: Indiana University Press, 1964. Also separately issued as *Terms for Order* and *Perspectives by Incongruity*. Selections from Burke's writings. Several of the listed dates of first publication are incorrect.

Language as Symbolic Action: Essays on Life, Literature, and Method. Berkeley and Los Angeles: University of California Press, 1966. Mostly criticism.

Collected Poems 1915–1967. Berkeley and Los Angeles: University of California Press, 1968.

The Complete White Oxen: Collected Short Fiction of Kenneth Burke. Berkeley and Los Angeles: University of California Press, 1968.

2. *Uncollected Items*

"La Baudelairienne," *The Sansculotte*, I (January, 1917), 9. Prose poem.

"The Allies of Humanism Abroad," *The Critique of Humanism*. Ed. C. Hartley Grattan. New York: Brewer and Warren, 1930, pp. 169–92.

"On Motivation in Yeats," *The Southern Review*, VII (Winter, 1941–1942), 547–61.

"Kinds of Criticism," *Poetry*, LXVIII (August, 1946), 272–82.

"Ideology and Myth," *Accent*, VII (Summer, 1947), 195–205.

"The Imagery of Killing," *The Hudson Review*, XIII (Spring, 1951), 151–67.

"A 'Dramatistic' View of Imitation," *Accent*, XII (Autumn, 1952), 229–41.

"Thanatopsis for Critics: A Brief Thesaurus of Deaths and Dyings," *Essays in Criticism*, II (October, 1952), 369–75.

"Symbol and Association," *The Hudson Review*, IX (Summer, 1956), 212–25.

"The Poetic Motive," *The Hudson Review*, XI (Spring, 1958), 54–63.

"Towards a Post-Kantian Verbal Music," *The Kenyon Review*, XX (Autumn, 1958), 529–46.

"On Form," *The Hudson Review*, XVII (Spring, 1964), 103–9.

"The Unburned Bridges of Poetics, or, How Keep Poetry Pure?" *Centennial Review*, VIII (Fall, 1964), 391–97.

"Dramatic Form—and: Tracking Down Implications," *Tulane Drama Review,* X (Summer, 1966), 54–63.

SECONDARY SOURCES

1. *Bibliographies*

FRANK, ARMIN PAUL, and MECHTHILD FRANK. "The Writings of Kenneth Burke: A Checklist." *Critical Responses to Kenneth Burke: 1924–1966.* Ed. William H. Rueckert. Minneapolis: University of Minnesota Press, 1969. Approximately 500 titles including anthologies.

RUECKERT, WILLIAM H. "Selected Bibliography of Works about Kenneth Burke." *Ibid.* Approximately 150 titles.

2. *Background Material Relating to Burke*

AARON, DANIEL. *Writers on the Left: Episodes in American Literary Communism.* New York: Harcourt, Brace & World, 1961. Study of communism's impact on American writers. A chapter treats Burke's contribution to the American Writers' Congress.

COWLEY, MALCOLM. *Exile's Return: A Literary Odyssey of the 1920's.* New York: Viking Press, 1951. Literary memoir by the earliest and closest of Burke's friends.

JOOST, NICHOLAS. *Scofield Thayer and "The Dial."* Carbondale: Southern Illinois University Press, 1964. Detailed, reliable history of the new *Dial.*

JOSEPHSON, MATTHEW. *Life Among the Surrealists: A Memoir.* New York: Holt, Rinehart & Winston, 1962. Memoir by another "exile" and friend of Burke's.

"Thirty Years Later: Memories of the First American Writers' Congress," *American Scholar,* XXXV (Summer, 1966), 495–516. Discussion by K. Burke, M. Cowley, G. Hicks, W. Phillips; D. Aaron, moderator.

WASSERSTROM, WILLIAM. *The Time of "The Dial."* Syracuse: Syracuse University Press, 1963. Assessment of the *Dial's* cultural contribution. Describes Burke as "*The Dial's* representative critic."

3. *Studies of Burke: Books*

HOLLAND, LAURA VIRGINIA. *Counterpoint: Kenneth Burke and Aristotle's Theories of Rhetoric.* New York: Philosophical Library, 1959. "There is nothing in Burke's rhetorical theory which is not implicit in Aristotle. In several respects, however, he has gone beyond Aristotle and made the implicit explicit."

KNOX, GEORGE. *Critical Moments: Kenneth Burke's Categories and Critiques.* Seattle: University of Washington Press, 1957. Useful but unsystematic short book. Knox is at his best when he elucidates Burkean terms by collating contexts in which they occur.

RUECKERT, WILLIAM H. *Kenneth Burke and the Drama of Human Relations.* Minneapolis: University of Minnesota Press, 1963. Concentrates on Burke's criticism but discusses it always in relation to the Dramatistic system which is excellently summarized in firm, broad outlines.

4. *Studies of Burke: Articles, Essays, Chapters of Books*

BEWLEY, MARIUS. "Kenneth Burke as Literary Critic," *Scrutiny,* XV (December, 1948), 254–77. Penetrating analyses of points of detail in which Burke goes amiss. But, as it sometimes slights the context, Bewley's wholesale dismissal of Burke's criticism is unjustified.

DUFFEY, BERNARD. "Reality as Language: Kenneth Burke's Theory of Poetry," *Western Review,* XII (Spring, 1948), 132–45. Reviews much of Burke's criticism from the Dramatistic point of view reached in the *Grammar of Motives.* Notes the transcendental split between symbolicity and physicality and concludes that Burke's is the fullest and most independent literary theory in existence.

DUNCAN, HUGH D. *Language and Literature in Society.* Chicago: University of Chicago Press, 1953.

DUNCAN, HUGH D. *Communication and Social Order.* New York: Bedminster Press, 1962. Duncan's books, Burkean in approach and containing long sections on him, together with Duncan's Introduction to the 1965 edition of *Permanence and Change,* illustrate the use made of Burke by a sociologist.

FERGUSSON, FRANCIS. "Kenneth Burke's *Grammar of Motives.*" *The Human Image in Dramatic Literature.* Garden City: Doubleday, 1957. Perceptive review which raises the issue of the nature of Burke's dramatistic dialectic.

FOGARTY, DANIEL, S. J. "Kenneth Burke's Theory." *Roots for a New Rhetoric.* New York: Teachers College, Columbia University, 1959. Attempt to assess Burke's place in a modern rhetoric.

FRAIBERG, LOUIS. "Kenneth Burke's Terminological Medium of Exchange." *Psychoanalysis and American Literary Criticism.* Detroit: Wayne State University Press, 1960. Reviews Burke's use of Freud from a somewhat restricted and clinical point of view.

FRANK, ARMIN PAUL. "The Reception of Kenneth Burke in Europe." *Critical Responses to Kenneth Burke: 1924–1966.* Ed. W. H. Rueckert. Minneapolis: University of Minnesota Press, 1969. Survey of European reactions to Burke.

GALLINO, LUCIANO. "Kenneth Burke e la Critica Americana," *Studi Americani,* III (1957), 315–46. Detailed but unfriendly treatment of Burke in terms of intellectual history. Defines his place among the American "conciliators" of scientific biologism and moral philosophy.

GLICKSBERG, CHARLES I. "Kenneth Burke: The Critic's Critic," *The South Atlantic Quarterly,* XXXVI (January, 1937), 74–84. Perceptive delineation of Burke's development from the 1920's to the 1930's, with specific emphasis on the influences on him.

GOMME, ANDOR. "Strategic Selection: Criticism by Choice of Terms." *Attitudes to Criticism.* Carbondale: Southern Illinois University Press, 1966. As in Bewley, penetrating, though at times derivative analyses of points of detail are used out of context to condemn the whole of Burke.

HYMAN, STANLEY E. "Kenneth Burke and the Criticism of Symbolic Action." *The Armed Vision: A Study of the Methods of Modern Literary Criticism.* New York: Alfred A. Knopf, 1948. Very informative and enthusiastic summary which praises Burke as the critic who comes closest to the ideal of inclusiveness.

NICHOLS, MARIE HOCHMUTH. "Kenneth Burke: Rhetorical and Critical Theory." *Rhetoric and Criticism.* Baton Rouge: Louisiana State University Press, 1963. In this chapter and in a 1952 article in the *Quarterly Journal of Speech,* Mrs. Nichols interprets Burke to students of speech and rhetoric.

OSBORN, NEAL J. "Toward the Quintessential Burke," *The Hudson Review,* XXI (Summer, 1968), 308–21. Assessment of *Towards a Better Life* and *Language as Symbolic Action* from the single perspective of a mature understanding of Dramatism.

PARKES, HENRY B. "Kenneth Burke." *The Pragmatic Test: Essays on the History of Ideas.* San Francisco: The Colt Press, 1941. Succinct survey of Burke's position in the late 1930's.

WARREN, AUSTIN. "Kenneth Burke, His Mind and Art," *The Sewanee Review,* XLI (1933), 225–36, 344–64. Well-balanced discussion of Burke's early fiction and criticism.

5. *Collections of Criticism*

RUECKERT, WILLIAM H., ed. *Critical Responses to Kenneth Burke: 1924–1966.* Minneapolis: University of Minnesota Press, 1969. Generous selection of criticism; bibliographies.

Index

The main entries in this index are *names of authors. Titles of works* appear as sub-entries under the name of the respective author. *Key terms of Burke's criticism* appear *en bloc* after his works. Other occurrences of these terms are also listed in order to clarify Burke's terminology by different or contrasting uses. The derivatives of names or terms have also been included. Thus, for instance, the entry "Aristotle" covers occurrences of "Aristotelian," "analogy" covers "analogical," etc. The "Notes and References" have not been indexed but may profitably be consulted for further occurrences of Burke's critical terms.